HOW

to write fiction like a pro

Robert Newton Peck

to write fiction like a pro

A simple-to-savvy toolkit
for aspiring authors

Maupin House

HOW to write fiction like a pro: A simple-to-savvy
toolkit for aspiring authors
By Robert Newton Peck
© 2006 Robert Newton Peck
All rights reserved.

Book Design: Mickey Cuthbertson
Cover Design: Josh Clark

Library of Congress Cataloging-in-Publication Data

Peck, Robert Newton.
  How to write fiction like a pro : a simple-to-savvy toolkit for
aspiring authors / by Robert Newton Peck.
    p. cm.
  ISBN 0-929895-85-1
  1. Authorship. I. Title.
  PN147.P357 2006
  808'.02--dc22
                                                          2005008272

🍎 **Maupin House**

Maupin House publishes professional resources for
K-12 educators. Contact us for tailored, in-school
training or to schedule an author for a workshop or
conference. Visit www.maupinhouse.com for free lesson
plan downloads.

The Robert Newton Peck Horse Video is available from
Tim Podell, 800-642-4181. Robert Newton Peck's website
is www.blahnik.info/rnpeck.

Maupin House Publishing, Inc.
PO Box 90148
Gainesville, FL 32607

800-524-0634
352-373-5588
352-373-5546 (fax)
www.maupinhouse.com
info@maupinhouse.com

10 9 8 7 6 5 4 3 2 1

Dedication

To my revered Miss Kelly who, on a dirt road and in a one-room schoolhouse, gave generations of barefooted scholars a university.

Table of Contents

HOW

"How?" asked Sitting Duck.

Many moons ago, lonely young brave longing to write love letter to faraway sweetheart, Mini Blanket, but smoke signals fail to soar like eagle in sunset.

Sitting Duck was stuck. At a loss for puffs.

This is HOW it all started. And it was Sitting Duck who led us in a charge of curiosity. Ever since, ambitious people have been asking HOW to do this, or HOW to handle that—or HOW to write a book.

A book is not written.

It is constructed.

You *build* a book, using raw materials and a toolkit. **HOW** shows you where to find the logs and *how* to build the cabin. And supplies you with the tools to use.

The most moronic question ever asked of an author is this one: "Where do you get your ideas?" Answer: First off, a book is not erected out of ideas. Quite the contrary. A good solid story is manufactured. Raw physical materials are sawed, hammered, sanded and shaped into a form by using the tools in a toolkit. Rather than an intellectual muse a fable is fabricated from fabric and fiber. Sweaty work performed on physical entities. Call it carpentry.

We got good news for y'all...**HOW** ain't professorial or textbooky. Instead, it is practical and professional. It clearly shows you *how* I do it. Please pardon the brag—I've done it (been published) sixty-five times. **HOW** will guide you to write fiction *not* like a prof but like a *pro*. With a whole set of useful tools.

How much hilarity we'll have together.

Learning isn't a load. It's laughter.

Don't Guess Who

Who?

This priceless little three-letter word is the most important pillar to support your story. You already know the answers to the easy W questions. Such as . . .

Where? A place you've lived in.

When? Pick a year you barely survived.

What? What happens. Don't worry about that just yet because your characters will decide that for you.

Why? Same as what. Later.

Who????? *Who* is in your story? You must definitely decide this prior to even thinking about writing page one. *Characterization* is the key to your success.

"Oh poor me," I can hear you wailing. "Do I really have to do *homework* before I attack my keyboard and reward the world with a fresh original opening? Such as . . . It was a dark and stormy night, the wind was whistling in his ears, and it was raining cats and dogs."

At that point, you'd sit there for a month, wondering what to type next, because you don't know *who* is in your story.

I have good news for you.

The homework's fun.

Think of several people who'll play parts in your drama. Who's making the scene? Let's say there are seven principal roles. We'll call one of them Stanley Livingstone. Start with a clean sheet of paper and begin listing everything you know about Stanley. You'll be amazed how *easy* this is.

How old is Stanley?

How old does he feel? (As I write this, I'm seventy-seven, and my motto is . . . "Never act your age.") Is Stanley tall, short, lean, or chubby? If so, just slightly chubby, or does he have more chins than a Hong Kong phone book? Is he rural or urban? Bright or stupid?

What does Livingstone do for a living? Does he do it well? Is he the CEO or a janitor? Establish if Stanley likes his work or dislikes it.

Single? Married? Divorced? Straight? Gay?

Hobbies? What's his favorite game? Does he collect stamps, store coupons, or beautiful blondes? Is he neat or is Stanley an unwashed, unshaven, unbarbered, smelly, gritty, grubby slob?

Okay, let's presume Stanley is married. Does he treasure his wife, Angela, but absolutely despise her nagging mother, Gargoyla? Can't blame him. Personally, I've never cared that much for Gargoyla ever since she overfed my goldfish and they all floated belly-up dead.

Important: In other words, always give somebody *reasons* for disliking someone.

At work, does Stanley fear or bootlick his boss, J. J. Bigdesk? Does he flirt with his leggy secretary, Fileen, who has the IQ of a Milky Way, thinks she invented the navel, and cannot simultaneously buff her nails and chew gum? Does he fret that she might be brighter than he?

Health. Is Stanley allergic? Frustrated? Constipated? What's in his medicine cabinet—a vast assortment of laxatives with product names that resemble hand grenades?

Does he swear? Pray? Would he throw a punch at someone who got him kicked off the company's bowling team? On the good side, I got a hunch that Stanley Livingstone takes his family to church, on Sundays when it's rainy and there's no golf. At noon, does he come home from church, take off his shirt, examine it, wondering if it's presentable enough to wear to the office on Monday morning?

Does he smell the shirt's armpit?

Yes!

We all have our little secrets. And as soon as Stanley secretly sniffs his shirt, *you strike gold!* You have a real human being. That's why we all watched Archie Bunker on television. To be sure, Archie wasn't fine or fancy; but oh boy, in his cruddy old clothes and beat-up chair—was he ever *real.* All over the country bumper stickers were shouting: "Tell 'em, Arch!"

When we looked at him we saw parts of ourselves.

He had virtues and vices.

Archie was human.

God bless men and women who get dirty at work. So rub some grease on your hero. Or manure. Beware of making him too goody-goody pure. He doesn't have to be a convicted felon, yet at least let's suspect he cheats at gin rummy.

What games does Stanley play?

If bright, chess.

If he's average, bridge. Or poker.

Or does he cheat at Bingo?

Once your Stanley sheet of paper is overflowing with his numerous traits, move on. You have seven characters, so perform this personality profile six more times. A competent author knows each character thoroughly. So deeply that he could flip

through *TV Guide* and tell which programs Stan
would watch or shun.

Next step.

Pretend a movie is being shot of your novel and you,
the author, have been flown out West to Hollywood.
Why? To assist the casting director regarding *who*
plays the part of Stanley. Wow! It's an actor you
worship. A manly guy named Wayne Lancaster Heston.
You already know how WLH walks and talks; so now,
as you're writing, Stanley becomes more vivid. More
alive. There's now fiber and texture in him.

In your mind, select an actor or actress for all seven
of your principals. Except you, whom you already
know. This imaginary casting session will aid in
making your characters real. And consistent! This is
a *must*.

Suddenly you become more than merely an
emerging author. Behold! You're a silver-screen
producer! You buy a beret. Change your name to
Otto or Cecil.

I told you this could be fun.

You Name It

Who?

Well, you and I established the importance of who in the first chapter. But we omitted a very prime element of personality.

What's the character's name?

Comedy and drama have diverse demands. In comedy, a writer is unwise to use just plain, ordinary names. And in drama, also unbright to use absurd names. As comedy is more fun, let's first take a look at humorous handles.

If your character is a big, dumb football coach, make his name big and dumb. We call him Bulkhead Beefjerky. Notice how we have so cleverly combined a naval term for a wall with a kind of dried food . . . producing a name that fits the fellow. For a football fullback we can't use Tarzan. Or can we? Yes, providing we add a nickname in front plus a winter sport suffix. Our result is Tank Tarzanski.

If Tank's main squeeze is sparkling and delicate, her name could well be Crystal Waterford. Now don't panic. The good people who market excellent

stemware called Waterford Crystal will have a sense
of humor and also welcome the free publicity.

Or, if she's the sweet silent type let's borrow a word
or two from our local supermarket and name her
Velveeta Mildcheddar.

Their biology teacher is Miss Eggplant.

A proud and pompous music director of a large high
school or college deserves at least three names. He's
much too uppity for merely two. Look! It's half-time. Out
on the gridiron he prances as a plumed and spangled
drum major, legs kicking seven feet in the air, a twirling
baton perhaps a good thirty above his toes.

Behold!

Dr. Humdrum Spitvalve Hornswoggle.

Notice how we combine (in order) boredom, part of a
brass instrument, and a dishonesty into a ridiculous
musician's name.

Where, you may be asking, do all of these names
come from? HOW do you find them?

Easy.

In your home.

At this very moment, you already possess a big book of nothing but nifty names. It's your telephone directory. A phone book. Do I use mine? You betcha! That's exactly where I happened to stumble across Fearless Ferguson, the daredevil in *Soup on Fire*. I looked under F. Two families. One was Fearless and the other was Ferguson. All I did was unite them.

In *Soup's Uncle*, my pal's visiting uncle is a very rough rowdy who arrives on a backfiring motorcycle. He is Soup's Uncle Vi. His full name is Virus Burdock, an infection and a weed. His motorcycle gang is The Hardboilers.

In a light operetta why not a tiny tenor with a booming voice—Trombonio. His enormous sopranic wife, twice his size, Tundra Rotunda, who might secretly be winking at a baritone, Cuspidoro Expectoranti.

Okay, enough already on the comedy.

Let's switch to drama. And please do note that even William Shakespeare and Charles Dickens employed ridiculous names. And they can *occasionally* be used for serious characters. For example, in a sleepy little Florida town it seems plausible to have a brawny, 260-pound chief of police yet with a gentle nature and even gentler name. Percival Sweetbutter in *Bro*.

Heedless to say, a high percentage of your people in a drama will demand ordinary (non-comic) names as they are just plain folks. And this includes your hero! So don't hype him with too romantic a name, like Tungsten Rampart.

Again, your telephone directory will supply you with a plenty of conventional names, to assist your avoiding using Mary Smith or Bob Jones.

Below are a few I found to use:

Branch Dockery	*Bro*
Yoolee Tharp	*Nine Man Tree*
Glory Callister	*Hallapoosa*
Greer O'Ginty	*Cowboy Ghost*
Tate Bannock Stonemason	*Extra Innings*
Tullis Yoder (hero)	*Horse Thief*
Thalia June Soobernaw	
Judah St. Jude (villain)	

Here's another tool for your now rapidly expanding toolkit. For names, try a thesaurus. Check the *diseases* and you'll maybe crack a smile. Trickanosis is a shady lady or perhaps a magician.

For an author, it's a hoot to slyly shoehorn a questionable name into a manuscript, to play a prank on your editor. Or your teacher. Here's one I sneaked into *Soup's Hoop*. A basketball team comprised of very tall men. Each player bore the nickname of Stretch—including Stretch Marx.

Crack open your thesaurus under *cheat* to revel in a romp of nifty names for law-firm partners: Swindle, Fleece, & Bilker.

A Northern dentist named Yank.
A female weightlifter . . . Hernia.

In your kitchen, reward yourself by taking a quick squint at a spice rack. Note the names. Which of your characters would they fit? You might consider having a sultry Paprika catch the wandering eye of Coriander.

Names will pop up everywhere.

At all times, best you carry a small notepad plus a golf pencil. Whenever you encounter an unusual lowercase noun (or word) that can double as a name, write it down. Do yourself a favor by doing yourself a list. In an elevator you just might see Otis. Often, even an uncomfortable name can trigger an eccentrically unique trait in your mind.

To help color a colorless character.

Plot

What's a plot?

The answer is pig simple.

One of the most common structures for a plot is two dogs and one bone.

If not a bone, try turf. Two armies battling to control one hunk of real estate. Most wars are fought over territory. Land stakes. Or maybe a bloodless battle, and these can be every bit as ruthless as a war. Let's say the president of a powerful Wall Street corporation has a heart attack and dies. Beneath him there are two subordinates, executive vice presidents, one a man and the other a woman. Do they want this top job? Do they ever! They'd eat their own young to get it.

Ah! Perhaps the bone is a funny bone. Again, a triangle. Let's imagine two men romantically involved with one woman who can't stomach either of them.

Or worse! A man between two women, Fistula and Vitriola. Like the bone, this unwise and unfortunate fellow is in deep doo-doo. Chewed to pieces.

As it is too painful to envision what horrors happen to a gentleman trapped between two ladies, let's switch to a more soothing scene. A bone and two dogs. Fido has it, but Rover wants it. We are not simple-minded socialists. Notice that we never toss half a bone to each dog. Doing so wouldn't ignite conflict. There has to be, in a novel, not quite enough meat to go around.

Not quite enough is the right amount.

I'll prove it. Imagine you're throwing a party. A gala. A big bash, to which you have invited exactly one-hundred guests. Everybody is here. So we play a party game.

Musical Chairs.

You place a hundred empty chairs in a circle, facing outward, and crank up the music. Everyone (except you) marches around and around, in no hurry. Why hustle? After all, there's a chair for every butt. Until! We remove one chair so there are ninety-nine seats and a hundred hinders. When the music suddenly stops some unlucky ozone hole will be seatless and ejected from the game. We continue, removing another chair and then another.

How does Musical Chairs finally end? Two tushes and one tuffet.

Two dogs. One bone.

This is only your start. Because a plot is a dramatic situation: Someone wants something, tries to get it, and is opposed. Fido's got a bone. But there's no exciting entertainment until Rover attempts to steal it and Fido resists.

Examine all of the personalities on your seven sheets of paper: A, B, C, D, E, F, and S . . . for Stanley.

Find someone who wants something. So intensely that he'll try anything to obtain it. Yet he is opposed. There must be hurdles in his path. Fences to leap over. Rivers to swim. A steep hill to climb.

As you read *Horse Thief*, you'll discover how seventeen-year-old Tullis Yoder steals thirteen horses destined for the slaughterhouse. And how, with the help of a lady doctor and an aging professional horse thief, he escapes the hot pursuit of crooks, three sheriffs, and a powerful judge to achieve his selfless purpose.

Remember this: The character who hungers for something can be someone other than Stanley. Is a banker eager to take his home? In the past mild-mannered Stanley hasn't been much of a scrapper. But somewhere, deep inside him, his backbone starts to stiffen, his muscles flex, and *nobody* is going to usurp his home from his family.

When it comes to holding what is rightfully his, friendly Fido can finally bear his fangs and become a fighter.

And a plot is born.

In conclusion, please permit my stressing once again that the principal ingredient in any plot is *want.* A character has to hunger for something, seek it, and in the process, overcome obstacles in order to attain it.

And it could be one dog after one bone.

My plots frequently are born when one of my key characters has a target. A goal.

Want is the key.

Car Crash

You be the judge . . .

Which of these phrases packs more punch?

> Back when Elizabeth was Queen of England.
> Or . . .When Elizabeth ruled.

Obviously *ruling* is far more potent than merely sitting on a throne and *being* a queen. Glancing back to 1600, Elizabeth Tudor *ruled!* Those who wouldn't be ruled were beheaded.

The above choice presents a fresh way to measure your own manuscript. And also something else. A pit stop. If you're still an upstart writer with a desire to be published someday, please allow my warning you to STOP before you plunge pell-mell into a puny and pathetic *pit*.

What pit?

Well, it is the vapid verb *to be.*

I am.	We are.	I was.
You are.	You are.	You were.
He is.	They are.	She was Queen.

These are actually all *ain'ts*. And I ain't gonna let you use 'em. For sound reason. Because if you describe what a character *is* or *was* you'll surely starve. Rather than telling me what he *is*, show me what he *does.* Action. He must *act. Do.*

Do what?

It's up to you whether he does something good or something bad. But if he does little or nothing, that is exactly what you shall deserve to earn as a professional writer. Little, or nothing.

Now for your car crash. Head on.

An entertaining story is sort of like a game of checkers. Or better yet, chess—as some characters are stronger and others weaker. At a chessboard of sixty-four squares two opponents face one another. Let's say they are Charlie and Marybelle. An amateur author might unwisely waste his time, as well as wasting a reader's time, describing what Charlie is wearing. A cowboy hat, a striped pajama top, Bermuda shorts, black socks, one Nike sneaker, and a red velvet bedroom slipper adorned with sequins.

The emerging writer feels oddly compelled to tell us that Charlie's hair is red and his eyes are blue. We readers are also uselessly informed that Charlie *is* a Methodist but used *to be* a Baptist, *is* in insurance, and frequently *is* yearning about learning to yodel. Charlie and Marybelle might sit facing each other for at least a decade.

But if neither makes a move, it is going to be one dreadfully dull chess game.

The cars have to crash.

An electric impulse must go leaping from anode to cathode to stir the stew and trigger the taste. We readers who are allowed to witness this chess match become interested when Charlie (playing white) makes his first move. Only a pawn, granted, but at least the combat has commenced.

This absurd example, however, does illustrate the distinct difference between what Charlie *is* (boring) and what he finally *does* . . .which is *attack.*

Marybelle must defend.

Because just coyly sitting there, *being there*, is nary enough. Which brings to mind a rather tedious stage play entitled *Hamlet.* I can't recall who wrote it, but an eternity of tiresome time is twiddled away by a passive prince who does nothing. He merely contemplates suicide as the entire audience wishes he'd commit so they could all get up, go home, flick on the TV, and watch *Bowling for Dollars.* However, there is one line in the play I clearly remember . . .

      "To be or not to be."

Now then, my advice to budding authors is as follows: *To be* is to avoid. So please make a note to yourself *not to be.*

At any public library in the United States you'll be able to locate my novel *Bro*. Read it for free. Until then, read this part of the story and discover how the hero, Broda Joe Dockery, eventually has to confront the cruel convict, Crit Zaggert. In literature, heads are not designed to think but to *butt*. (In Elizabeth's court, *roll*.)

It was Zaggert. The Critter.

Cuffed hands held a raised bullhorn. A voice spoke.

Spooky. Like the hiss of a snake. "Girlie Face, you in there?

Show yourself. Come out with both hands on top a yo pretty head. You hear me?"

Aunt Lulu gasped.

Branch did a plenty more.

Broda Joe heard a sharp click clack as Grampap levered a cartridge into the firing chamber of his aging Winchester.

Glancing to his right, Bro saw its steely muzzle poke forward, out an upstairs window. Without delay, the rifle fired. The camp truck's windshield shattered. Inside it, somebody in the passenger seat cussed and shot a pistol. Twice.

"Branch!" Aunt Lulu screamed.

Grampap moaned as he lost control of the Winchester.

The rifle fell, clattering down the rough shingles of the slanted porch roof, to smack the stony walkway.

Seeing it, Zaggert started forward. But he was thirty feet distant and both his ankles were hobbled by a short chain.

Broda Joe didn't pause to think. Diving out of the window, he rolled down the roof's steep incline, and fell onto the stones.

His shoulder hit with a thud. He felt a bone break. More than one, and the cracking pains pierced into him, deeper than daggers.

Hurt to breathe. And he tasted blood.

Crawling to the rifle, he noticed its trigger housing had worked loose. The Winchester was broken and couldn't fire.

Nonetheless, Bro forced himself to crouch, almost stand, and point the rifle at Crit Zaggert. He wouldn't git took alive.

Broda Joe Dockery wasn't returning to Hell.

He chose Heaven.

Fiction ain't dreary description. Contrarily, it's an eventual head-on collision of two opposing forces. In earlier chapters you have thoroughly established who they *be;* not by numbing nomenclature but by how each behaves.

Behavior is your deftest descriptive device. It increases the speed and force of each of two cars to augment the ultimate . . .

A car crash!

Talk It Up

Talk. Talk. Talk.

Too often, we human beings have a tendency to do more talking than thinking. More talking than working. Read any of my novels and you'll see many a page that is chiefly comprised of conversation. In a book it's called dialogue. And there's a secret to writing dialogue that sounds genuine and rings true.

What is the secret?

You see, a number of emerging authors try to create a conversation between two stick figures, A and B.

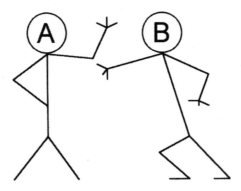

What does A say to B?

Not even a genius like Mr. Thomas Alva Edison could answer that question. Why not? Because we know neither A nor B. Now you see why we began my book by reading a chapter entitled "Don't Guess Who." Ah! You are suddenly aware of the secret of writing good dialogue, and it is this. Again, do your homework.

Know who's talking!

Let's pretend that you are inventing a conversation between two people. Billy-Bob is a boy. April-June May is a girl. The emerging writer commits a major blunder if he constantly uses these names when he doesn't have to. For example:

> "Yo trousers is muddy, Billy-Bob."
> "So's your mussed-up calico dress, April-June May."
> "You's still the cutest little ol' boy in near to about all of Hawg Holler, Billy-Bob Bodeen. No wonder I couldn't resist rassling with you here in the mud."
> "And you's a right ripe gal, April-June, and a good rassler."

Absurd. But my point is plain. How senseless and boring to repeat the first names. By the content of what is said, a reader easily tells who is speaking. Unless, of course, April-June appears often in trousers and Billy-Bob wears a dress.

Get earnest about learning how to write dialogue by reading this awkward kissing scene in which Rob is introduced to the game Smooch in *Soup in Love*.

Light comedy.

Entering the parlor, I spotted Norma Jean Bissell, and instantly suspected (from the beckoning gleam in her eyes) that Smooch had little or nothing in common with baseball. Infield or outfield.

We boys talked about baseball a lot.

Never about Smooch, or anything at all like it . . .

So I approached Norma Jean with extreme caution, to face whatever lay in store.

Or run away.

"Okay," sighed Norma Jean.

"Okay?" I asked.

"Yes," she said quietly. "Do it."

Do it?

I was willing to try anything once, including when I attempted to bat lefty, instead of righty. Hitting left is no cinch.

"I'm . . .not a . . .really not a . . ."

"Not a what?"

"I'm not a lefty."

"A . . .whaty?"

"You know," I quickly explained. Girls are so thick-witted about some things that you have to go really slow whenever you try to clarify anything in detail. "I'm . . . uh. . .not left-handed."

Norma Jean flinched. "And what's that supposed to mean?"

"Well . . .uh. . .I'm a righty. If I was a lefty, maybe I'd play first. But seeing as I'm born the way I am, I won't get to first base."

"Not," said Norma Jean, "at the speed you're going."

"I've never played before."

"No kidding."

I nodded.

"Neither has Soup," I said, feeling my

underwear begin to itch. "Have you ever noticed," I asked her, "that some people are better, at a certain kind of game, than others?"

"Oh, have I ever!"

On a more serious note, in *Extra Innings* a great-grandfather and a young boy have taken a most treasured dog for her final outing. Abbott, the old gentleman, cannot bring himself to pull the trigger. Thus, this conversation with his great-grandson.

Tate approached to stare straight into his great-grandfather with sober blue eyes that already knew and understood. Never had Abbott seen Tate Bannock Stonemason appear so full-fledged. How ironic, this day of mixed blessing.

"So that's why you brought the Ruger."

Abbott nodded.

"You're intending to shoot her."

"No. You are."

"Me?"

"You. Because I have homed and hunted with her for a decade. We can't ask Viddy to perform this, yet, having discussed it, I know we have her reluctant approval. As you're the stocky bull calf of our herd, you are nominated."

With a gentle hand on a young shoulder, he asked, "Can you do it?"

"Yes," Tate said without hesitation. "Because it has to be done. You and Aunt Vidalia aren't the only cognizant people. I've noticed. And it's heartrending to watch Ballerina falter. If I call her name, she doesn't always hear. And when a chair is

relocated, sometimes she'll bump into it.
Every step hurts. Her moaning is a plea for
help." Tate swallowed. "One of us ought to
rescue her."

"It's a lot to ask of you, Tater."

"She's a lot of dog."

Be aware that this interchange isn't just talk
because—and note this carefully—*something is
either happening or is fixing to soon happen.*

Moral: Allow the speech to inform a reader which
person is speaking. First, do your homework, and
know who's talking; then it's a cinch for you, an
author, to write what they say.

Twins

Tweedledee and Tweedledum.

More than a century ago, some obscure cartoonist drew twins, a couple of fat-faced, unfunny fellows who became the symbols of sameness. Exactly alike. No one could tell one from the other. Result? Dee and Dum were deadly dull.

Beware this trap.

Editors tell me that countless manuscripts for children's books are rejected because two kiddy characters are too much alike. Clones instead of clowns.

A marvelous motion picture entitled *Twins* was charming, amusing, and entertaining. The twins were completely different. Arnold Schwarzenegger and Danny DeVito. Variety personified. Although a comedy, this movie managed to be both sensitive and caring. Its success was based on twins that were the antithesis of one another. Direct opposites.

Every so often on TV, ancient black-and-white comedy movies are aired, flickeringly funny, and starring two very successful comedians.

Stan Laurel and Oliver Hardy.

Were they alike? Hardly. Stan Laurel was short, slender, shy—and more silent than his large lump of a companion, Oliver Hardy, who posed as the bossy boss. The know-it-all. Had this comedy team been two Laurels or two Hardys, they would have failed and never achieved nationwide fame.

Let's get serious.

Take a minute or two to evaluate both personalities of a pair of men that weren't a bit funny.
However, they were far more famous than the two slapstickers.

Sherlock Holmes and Doctor Watson.

Not at all alike.

Holmes was the mastermind, a brilliant detective who eventually solved the mystery; and just in the nick of time, collared the culprit. In each story, it was always Holmes who abruptly announced: "Let's go, Watson! We must await outside the third oaken door of Contessa Capozzola's castle as the graveyard's clock tower strikes the twelve tones of midnight."

Do the readers know why?

No, and neither does Watson, as he represents us readers, asking Holmes the very questions we would ask. Watson is as baffled as we are, especially earlier, as Holmes discovers a dead black widow spider inside Sir Rodney Cuthburton's ear trumpet. At tea time. Needless to add, their creator, Sir Arthur Conan Doyle, was wise enough not to portray two John Watsons or two detectives like Sherlock Holmes.

Learn from the masters, like Sir Arthur.

And maybe a bit from me.

Fourteen of my *Soup* series books were profitably published in paperback and hardcover. Now, you should ask, what was the spine of their success? They certainly weren't about mature British sleuths. Instead, merely two half-grown Vermont boys on neighboring farms. Soup and Rob.

Were they two peas in a pod? One might suspect that the boys are almost identical. Wrong!

Luther Wesley Vinson, whose nickname was Soup, is the detonator, a percussion cap, the spark plug who ignites the action, usually a prank that somehow goes awry, plunging the boys into trouble.

Robert Newton Peck is Rob, who tells the story, the narrator. A year and four months younger than Soup, he is far more cautious. His role is the recording secretary. In real life, I recall always playing Boswell to Soup's Johnson. As in this barn-painting scene from *Soup for President.*

> "Make a mark," yelled Soup, hands cupped to his mouth, "right up where your left hand is."

"Why?"

"Because that's where the S in Soup ought to start."

"Are you sure we have enough paint?"

"It's only four letters," said Soup.

"I can spell."

"Did you mark the spot?"

"Yes," I said, not quite daring to look up at the white scribble of chalk that I had added to Mr. Cyrus McGinley's property.

"Okay," said Soup, "now reach up with your right hand and mark it, so you'll know how wide to make the top of the S."

Eyes closed, I chalked another squiggle.

"That's good enough."

"Soup . . ."

"Yeah?"

"I'm not sure that painting your name on Mr. McGinley's barn is such a hotdog of an idea."

"Why not? It pays to advertise."

"Well. Because I don't think it'll help you win."

"You're not supposed to think."

"What am I supposed to do?"

"Paint."

"Your uncle is going to get sore, Soup."

"Nah. Uncle Charlie is a regular guy."

Soup was busy with a large screwdriver and a chisel. Sitting on the apple-strewn ground, he began to pry up the lid from a gallon of red paint that he'd "borrowed" from his uncle's tool shed earlier that morning.

"Ya know, Rob, that S ought to be bigger."

"I want to get down."

"You just got up there."

"I still want to climb down off this ladder."

"You're not up very high. It's only a twenty-footer."

"Maybe it doesn't look so high from down where you are. From up here, it looks like one heck of a drop."

"You'll get used to it."

"What's underneath me?" I asked Soup.

"Something soft."

"Like what?"

"Manure."

"Oh, no! If I fall myself off this dumb ladder and land in a manure pile, Mama will kill me. And if she doesn't, Aunt Carrie will."

"They won't kill you."

"How come?"

Soup laughed. "The fall will."

Zany, yet it worked. Several of the *Soup* books were produced as TV shows on ABC's *Weekend Specials.*

Advice: Read a *Soup* adventure or two in order to understand clearly how Soup's personality differs from mine, Rob's. He was a leader. I, merely the reluctant follower. It's preposterous to believe that Soup became a minister, yet he truly did, claiming that he'd been ordained at birth. What else can a boy become who is named Luther Wesley Vinson?

For your edification, take a quick look at a few other teams of two individuals that vary:

Bud Abbott and Lou Costello
Mutt and Jeff
An odd couple: Felix Unger and Oscar Madison
Dean Martin and his partner
Mork and Mindy

When you create two characters who will closely
relate as active associates, ensure that they differ!
Harpo ain't Chico ain't Groucho.

Writing is art is beauty is *variety*.

Why is your early morning alarm clock so ugly, so
abrasive to hear? Because it has no variety. Not in
tone, volume, or texture of sound. Just a grating and
annoying buzz. Contrast it to a symphony orchestra
composed of strings, woodwinds, brasses, and
percussion (anything that is struck). The tiny tinsel
ting of a triangle is nothing at all like a booming
bass drum. Nor does the haunting, reedy oboe
resemble a trombone.

Ergo, in an orchestra, it is truly the variety that pleases
our ears and lifts our spirits. One sort of a sound
differing from another. The charm of contrast.

In your book, beware the fatal error of creating
identical twins like Tweedledee and Tweedledum.

The Camera

In every book, there is a camera.

No, not one that *takes* pictures. This one *gives* pictures to your readers. Your camera is not a physical entity. Yet it exists. And there's only *one.*

Where? Behind the eyes of one (or more) of your characters. Always inside somebody's head.

Warning: Your camera is *never* aimlessly floating in the air as though searching for a place to roost. This happens when an author decides that he or she will *tell* the story. Won't work. That's a no-no. The camera may shift from one character to another, but it is always anchored. Bolted into place.

Editors call this viewpoint. Or point of view.

Whichever. The reader must constantly be aware that the camera is behind the eyes of one certain being, seeing what he sees, hears, smells, tastes, and feels. The camera will, however, show us what other characters are doing, yet always seen through the eyes of the character who is, at this moment, the photographer.

Some books are written strictly from one point of view. For example, in all of the Soup books, there are two very active boys. But all action is seen through Rob's eyes. Never through Soup's.

In *A Day No Pigs Would Die*, the camera is behind only Rob's eyes. No one else's. Ditto for its sequel, *A Part of the Sky*.

For contrast, I strongly urge you to read *Horse Thief* or *Bro.* In both novels, there's still only one camera, but it shifts positions. Behind one character's eyes, and then, in a following chapter, behind someone else's. This we call a plural (rather than singular) viewpoint.

Question . . . How do you, an author, decide which to use, a singular or plural point of view?

Here's *how* I make this choice. If my protagonist, my hero, is going to be present at every event in the entire novel, one viewpoint is adequate. We keep the camera in our hero's head (not in mine!) throughout. But if the hero is absent from a particular scene, we have to transfer the camera to the head of someone else.

For example . . . Our hero is Harold Heroic.

A nice guy, yet Harold has enemies. If everyone likes him, we sure do have a boring, ho-hum story. So there are, I regret to report, a couple of evil entities who are conspiring to do him dirt. Their names are . . .

Hold it! Better check my thesaurus under evil, filthy, criminality. Ah. Got it. The thugs are: Pug and Pillory. See how easy that is?

Now to continue . . . Late at night, seated at a dimly-lit table in a dingy dive, our pair of punks lays plans to harm Harold. One is large, the other is small. Seeing as huge Pug is the palooka, the muscle, and a big bully, his gun moll Pillory is dominant—and *inside her head* our camera now functions. Simple. Do remember that the camera records what is said and what is done by both parties. Yet we readers discover only the secret feelings of Pillory, not Pug.

In a following chapter, we are no longer in the sudsy saloon, and are behind the eyes of Harold's devoted mother as she bakes him cookies. And later, with Harold's well-fed girlfriend, Suette, who is now gazing at Harold and wishing he'd floss away a hunk of pizza pepperoni that is lodged in the larger-than-normal gap between his front teeth. It's been there for a week.

That is her point of view.

Show Biz

How did this craft of writing begin?

With art. Here's my assumption. It started half a million years ago, when we hairy humans lived in caves. Prior to language. Early man only pointed at objects and grunted.

Imagine a cave's gloomy interior. The male is prone, asleep, his pillow is a rock only slightly softer than his head. The woman, who even back then couldn't tolerate seeing a man loafing, kicked him awake, handed him his club, and then prodded him out of their cave and into bad weather. No doubt gesturing that she and her offspring were hungry. Then as now, "When Mama ain't happy, ain't *nobody* happy."

A day or two later, Hairy Harry returned, battered and bloody, but dragging a dead animal which they ate raw, or half-roasted.

That evening, his woman and children were sleeping by the fire, their bellies full of meat that he had provided. Nothing makes a male so proud, or stand so tall, than realizing he was a good hunter. Before going to sleep that night, this hairy man who knew no words did one more thing.

On the wall of his cave, using a sharp stone, Hairy

drew himself, his mate, his young ones, a fire,
and one or two animals he had seen that day. To
record his story. At that moment he established the
primitive but prime rule of writing.

Don't *tell* the story.

Show it!

Writing is *show business.*

The secret is tangibility. Avoid writing about
someone's feelings. Write about *stuff.* Things.
Objects. Something that can be drawn by a pebble or
photographed by a high-priced camera.

If you have written something and wonder if
it's worthwhile, here's the test . . . can it be
photographed?

If it can't, rip it into small pieces, and then rewrite it
until someone can *see it.* People don't want to open
your book, or mine, and read it—because we no
longer live in a word generation. Today is a *screen*
generation. We have become watchers.

Folks want to open a book and *watch it happen.*

How do you, the eager, emerging writer, accomplish
this? Easily. I'll help you. Let's compose two lists.
One will be our intangible list of useless words that
cannot be photographed. Our second list will be
merely a collection of stuff. But visible.

Intangible	Stuff
Love	Dog
Caring	Horse
Hate	Knife
Nervous	Ballpoint pen
Dream	Boot
Worry	Cowboy hat
Heartbreak	Teapot

Perhaps the chief reason that I have been published sixty-five times is because I don't write about feelings. I show my readers *stuff*. Not being a moralist, I avoid what people ought to do and merely show a reader what someone is *doing*. Not what he's feeling. After all, who in heck cares about what somebody else is going through?

To wit . . . Melissa LaMope was in the quiet of her lonely room, in torment. Suffering. She felt shattered. Betrayed. Wondering, wailing, worrying if Steve Scumbag would ever come back.

Not if he's got any sense. Keep going, Steve. You are well rid of this boring babe. She's much too intangible to bother with. Or write about.

What is Melissa's basic problem?

It's this: Her level of happiness depends on what Steve thinks of her. Steve Scumbag probably is now seated in a sports bar, burping beer, loudly commenting on a game called football about which he knows nothing. Blessed with the IQ of a jellybean, Steve hasn't had a thought in ten years. And she cares what *he thinks*?

Instead, show Melissa's strengthening, involving herself in a sport, a camera club, or a rugged outdoor hike. Have her tightening the laces of her L.L. Bean trail-climbers with resolute tugs that represent (show!) fortitude.

Let's play a very rudimentary game.

It's called Show and Tell.

The difference between the two shall become very clear to you, and this difference is a cinch to savvy. To see.

"Bill was nervous." This sentence is an absolute failure because it has no picture, It weakly *tells* the story.

Instead, let's *show* the story . . .

"Bill was clicking his ball-point pen, on and off, on and off."

What's good about this? It's action that readers can see and hear. There's *stuff* in this picture. A hand, a pen, and some motion, even the subtle sound of a clickety-click.

Okay, but let's not be so satisfied that we stop right there. What say we sharpen and strengthen our scene. "Sitting on a hard bench outside the principal's office, Bill was peeling the skin along the edge of his thumb as raw red flesh began to show. Until he could gnaw the flesh between his teeth, rip it away, and taste the hot sweetness of his own blood."

Learn this: Not all pictures are pretty.

But if you really want to become a competent author, do not tell the story. Don't tell me that Bill is nervous. Show me Bill's thumb. A torn, bleeding thumb will show readers all of Bill at that particular moment. You won't use pictureless words—like *nervous*. It's a loser.

Years ago, I taught an evening adult-education course on *how* to write. Forty people were asked to submit a brief, neatly-typed sample of their work.

Of the few who dared, almost all manifested limited ability—their stories too long. Wordy. One captured my attention. A single paragraph, untyped, scrawled on blue-lined notebook paper featuring a trio of torn holes. This writer, a graying and matronly lady, had actually printed a title atop her meager offering:

TEAPOTS

Three teapots sit on my kitchen shelf. Come visit me. We'll share Constant Comment from the lavender pot with yellow butterflies. On weekday mornings it's plain Lipton in the gray stoneware. My third teapot has never brewed tea. Margaret, our only child, gave it to me when she turned nine, on the last Christmas of her life.

Somehow it broke. We spent our holidays
with string and glue, piecing it together.
Parts of the handle and spout are missing. I
will let you read in our tea leaves which of
my teapots is truly mine.

"Teapots" is a pearl of purity. Strong, simple, and sweet, it represents the way Robert Newton Peck would write, if he only had her talent.

Important: Please note that it avoids pictureless words, such as *tragedy* or *heartbreak.* Instead, it is a devotion to physical objects. Tangible stuff. For some weird reason, I can't explain just why, we sometimes grow up believing that *love* and *care* are such wonderful words. Keep using them in your story and they'll really get you somewhere.

To the poorhouse.

Example: "The farmer had a horse. He *loved* his horse very much and always took good *care* of his horse."

Is this good writing? No. It's blah. There is no picture. Nothing tangible for a reader to look at.

How about this? "Bending low, Benjamin hefted a heavy hoof to cradle gently between his knees. His hands were occupied with tools, yet as he worked on Betsy's hoof, he softly rubbed his head against her massive flank to quiet his mare from the fear."

Hey! Get the picture?

Whether you write for kids or grown-ups, the process is the same. Give a reader some *stuff* to watch. Just for fun, another example. I would have starved to death had I written like so: "Janice Riker was a very mean little girl who did *mean* things to me, and I will always *hate* Janice." *Mean* and *hate* are intangible words (pictureless) and every bit as useless as *care* and *love.*

How about this? "It was Saturday morning. We were playing Cowboys and Indians and I was helplessly tied to a tree. Along came Janice. She yanked down my britches and sang: 'I got a hornet. I got a hornet.'"

Now *that's* a picture. Lots of stuff to watch. To *show.*

To make *you* a writer.

Power Tools

Physics.

In brief, it's entity plus energy. To use simpler terms, physics is sort of a study of stuff (physical objects) and how it behaves. Matter in motion.

For aspiring writers, a solid course in physics is more beneficial than ten semesters of poetry. Why? Because powerful prose (or possibly a poem with punch) is based on at least one specific item, a *thing*, and what it does—or *how* a human hand handles it.

What things are we considering?

Well now, with polite apologies to Sears and also Black & Decker—*power tools*. The tool doesn't have to be a thirty-pound sledgehammer. It can be a sewing needle that weighs a fraction of an ounce.

Here's an example. In my novel *Cowboy Ghost*, inexperienced sixteen-year-old Titus Timothy MacRobertson, must convince his domineering father—and himself—that he's as much of a man as his older brother, Micah. In chapter two, Titus has tried to rope a tough mustang horse and gets his young body bruised and beaten. Cut. He needs stitches. The strong-willed and gray-haired housekeeper, Mrs. Krickitt, has known him since infancy and helped raise him. His rear end happens to be the area requiring thread, *but* (no pun intended) he resists removing his trousers.

"Snake off your belt, Tee."

"No how. All due respect, I'm certain not going to expose my personal self half naked in front of you."

"Sixteen year ago, you was entire naked on the night I attended your birthing." She unhitched his jeans. "That ornery outlaw of a horse near about peeled you like a potato. Amazing you're still breathing."

Actual, I was holding my breath every time her cussed needle punctured my flesh, and also when the thread got pulled.

"No more," I told her.

"Mind your business," she snapped. "For thirty-five years, these needles of mine pierced and patched a regiment of ranch hands. Those that got ripped at honest work. And, in the wee hours, more'n a few that aspired to become the dumbest drunk in town at The Bent Ace."

To prove her disapproval our veteran housekeeper yanked a stitch a tug tighter than needed.

I was sprawled sunny-side-up across her lap and cooking apron. Hardly a position of dignity.

"Hey, go easy!" I yelped. "You aren't roping a broomtail. I'm Titus, in case you forgot. Can't admit I cotton to display a bare bottom in front of somebody of the female persuasion."

Bending, she whispered to my ear. "Who do you think soaped that uppity behind of yours when you were a babe? Then powdered your particulars with cornstarch? Before that, your big buffalo of a brother. Plus the embroidery I've pricked into ten score of bunk busters, in all sections of their anatomies. North and south."

"Is that so?" I knew it was.
Mrs. Krickitt nodded. "I've observed more
naked male flesh than a dozen of The Bent Ace
hostesses. And," she huffed, "I can't favor of
having been charmed by even a sacred square
inch of the view."
It hurt me to laugh. But every stitch cried.
She certain could yank her thread.

In the above scene, a needle does far more than sew.
It establishes character. Two distinct personalities.
A tough-talking yet deeply caring housekeeper who
is tending young Titus whom she has always loved
as though he were her very own child. Without the
needle, which is the physical object connecting the
pair of people, there wouldn't be such an intimate
association. A few knots of thread tie the pair
together—as they truly belong.

Leaving a little needle behind (or in one), let's now
examine another metallic implement, one beyond
gigantic, and capable of crushing out life in less than
a tick of time . . .

Page 1 of my novel *Bro.*

The first two paragraphs of the prologue:

A giant hissing snake of steel and steam.
Half a mile in length, the black serpent began to
slither forward, spurred by the engineer's oily
glove on her throttle.
A chain of couplings snapped into contact
with a series of metallic clanks. Gradually,
the great locomotive lurched forward, gaining
ground, increasing her speed. Above the

arrowhead prow, her Cyclops eye pierced the inky darkness with a lance of light. The wheels of forty-four freight cars, each weighing more than one hundred tons, turned faster and faster. The charging train became a curving bullwhip of iron and power, able to demolish anything and anyone in her path.

Above, we have a huge physical entity—yet like the housekeeper's needle, it is also active. And more, the prologue serves to set the entire story in motion as a detonating device. An early-on hand grenade that explodes to begin a novel's war.

In summary, to become a powerful writer, constantly introduce yourself to the tools (and weapons) of power. Some are small. Others large. You'll discover just *how* potent tangible articles can be. A large locomotive or a tiny needle.

Groom your work. Try to avoid sentences that are dedicated to the non-physical—such as ideas, concepts, thoughts, dreams, emotions. Rather than telling a reader what a character is *feeling*, show me what he/she is doing, *and with what!* An empty hand can too often portray a rather vacant story—unless it's a fist. Put a tool or weapon in somebody's fingers. *Grip*—and you'll write grippingly.

Pen power is physics.

So get physical.

Discipline

Kids, listen up to your old Uncle Rob.

When you first write something original (be it a song, short story, poem, or a joke), please be aware that the piece is not yet in its final form. Because it needs grooming.

It's only a first draft.

Even at my age and with all my experience as a published author, whenever I mail a fresh, new manuscript to New York City, to Random House or to HarperCollins, I can predict for sure and certain that my editor will require my rewriting most of the book a second time. And—don't faint—possibly even a touch-up third.

Good writing means rewriting.

So hear me loud and clear. When a teacher thinks that the piece you have written is good enough to spend more time and effort on, this is always *good news*. It doesn't mean that what you wrote is poor. Not in the least. If the teacher suggests that you improve it—do it! Do not moan and groan or pout like a lazy spoiled brat.

Every girl knows that washing her hair is not enough. That's only step number one. Her hair also has to be dried and then brushed. As we said above, it has to be groomed.

Polished.

Ditto for attending a party. It ain't going to fly if all you do is dress up and wear fancy clothes. At the party, you also have to manifest manners. Good manners. The kind that polish you so's you'll shine like a new penny.

Hold it!

Is all this just a bunch of empty chatter?

Stop right now and think. Just imagine if I told one of my editors, "I refuse to rewrite and *groom* my novel, and you people up there in New York City can go to heck and keep the nice big pile of money that you're eventually promising to pay me."

I'd be nuts to do such.

Crazy.

So please learn *this* early in your young life: Discipline is expected from each and every one of us. Don't wince at the word. Okay, so maybe you're slightly frowning. Why? Because at your age, dreary discipline comes charging at you, again and again, from so many different directions. From your mother, father, grandparents, aunts, uncles, older cousins. Also from your teachers, your minister, and maybe when and if you misbehave, from a cop. Or a coach.

Handle it!

But remember this. And smile...

The best discipline in your entire world does *not* come from someone else. It is born within *you*. In your brain. What is it called?

Self-discipline.

Over half a century ago, in a very rural Vermont one-room school, Miss Kelly (who taught us grades first, second, third, fourth, fifth, and sixth) did not waste her time, or ours, on dispensing the false value known as "giving students self-esteem." What rot.

Instead, she taught us to manage ourselves, to control our own conduct, to weigh in our very own minds the difference between right or wrong.

And from *self-discipline* came our awakening awareness of self-esteem. Inside, we began to realize that we were decent, and diligent, willing to work at school and handle a lot of farm chores at home. Every day.

Do you wonder *how* I finally matured from that little one-room mountain school to becoming a successful author? Of course you're curious. So many of your letters to me ask: "*How* did you become an author?"

It began with a teacher.
Miss Kelly, who first gave us discipline. Not by her ruler that whacked us when we deserved it, but by believing in us—so that eventually we started to believe in ourselves.

That's really the only discipline that counts.

The one inside your *self*.

That gives you the gumption to write and rewrite—to *groom*—your work until it's the best you can make it.

Little Words

What?

You bought a thesaurus? A word-finder?

Offhand, I'd have to admit that's a sensible move, as I use a thesaurus upon occasion and it comes in handy. As I said earlier in "You Name It." However, as you are well aware, some things can be abused:

> Alcohol, if you over-imbibe.
> Cell phone, if you talk while you drive.
> Driver's license, when you run a red light.

An amateur author (or rather, an emerging one, and let's name him Elmer Emerging) can abuse a thesaurus. How? Constantly trying to gussy up his prose by erasing a plain word and then inserting one that's fancy. Or adding words that are totally unnecessary.

Let's look at an example of Elmer's writing:

"Here come the Indians," said Custer.
Oh my golly, Elmer thinks. Has he already used the word *said* twenty chapters ago, and now he's repeating it, and book reviewers will attack his castle with rakes, hoes, and burning torches? What

does Elmer do? The wrong thing. Quickly he erases *said*, consults his thesaurus for a synonym, smiles, and zaps in a substitute. One that sounds stronger to poor Elmer's tone-deaf ear.

"Here come the Indians," Custer *exclaimed.*

Well, now that he's sullied his sentence to sorry, is Elmer satisfied? Heck no. He's determined to frilly it up even worse. How? (And this has nothing to do with Indians). By adding overused exclamation points! Plus an absolutely useless -*ly* adverb.

"Here come the Indians!" Custer exclaimed *excitedly!*

Picture this. There stands Custer with a few fellow troopers of the Seventh Cavalry, casually observing that 3,000 war-painted Sioux are galloping in his direction, whooping, and in one minute are fixing to eat his face.

Just how excited is Custer?

Only the Little Big Horn Hand Laundry will learn.

As an author, one who confesses that he has committed every mistake possible, I've discovered that if one employs *little words* instead of big impressive ones, and uses these little words well, a story becomes clear and strong. No need to show off a pretentious vocabulary.

Twenty centuries ago, in a far-away, ancient land, an

uneducated yet magnificent Nazarene carpenter told his parables in humble words. A beggar beside the road. A woman at a well. A camel through the eye of a needle. A mustard seed. How small is the seed of mustard? Smaller than the period that finishes this sentence.

Yes, a thesaurus is sometimes useful. But I betcha that *you* already know all of the words you'll ever need.

One word can rescue a blah sentence. The sentence you just read, obviously, has not been saved. In fact, it's sinking. Dull. So let's give it another go: *Gussy up* a sentence.

Here are examples of how a single word can be the *buzz word* to make a sentence shine:

An awkward term to *hopscotch* a reader's eye.
The *swagger* of success.
A *strut* of confidence.
The sun, a *golden gong* of morning...using the unexpected noun that is stronger than any adjective. It doesn't quite fit. A sun is not a musical instrument any more than the moon is food. But when a full midnight moon is a *silver wafer*, your sentence sparkles.
The wrong of it (like the gong of it) reads so right.

How about these:

> One flashing *red light* of guilt.
> Dark clouds *breeding* weather.
> The stinging *swat* of insult.
> Fistula was the belle of the *brawl.*

You already know a lot of terms to employ as buzzers. All it takes is a bit of thought.

A *trinket* of time.

Cliché.

It is pronounced klee shay.

What's it mean? Usually a cliché is a blah, bland, boring, tiresome phrase that is dull, stale, not fresh. It is "run-of-the-mill" and also "dry-as-dust."

Words for the witless.

Overused.

Below are a few yawning examples:

> It was raining cats and dogs.
> I was beside myself. Worn to a frazzle.
> He acted in the nick of time.
> So hungry I could eat a horse.
> Ran as fast as his legs could carry him.
> Snow white. Sky blue. Green as grass.
> The night was pitch black.
> I'm feeling in the pink.
> Happy as a clam.

We all unthinkingly use clichés when we talk to one another. They pop out. In conversation they can be forgiven. Not in print!!! As you review today what you typed yesterday, please do concentrate on spotting and removing (be a spot remover) trite, ho-hum clichés and replace them with originality.

Creative writing isn't merely a term.

It deserves to be practiced.

Give me *new*.

If you haven't ever cracked open a Bible and have no idea whatsoever how it even begins, allow my filling you in. In the book of Genesis, the very first verb, the first action word you read, is the fifth word.

"In the beginning God *created* . . ."

Wasn't a copycat.

Did something fresh and inventive.

Good going, God.

So, if you will please permit, do dig up a dose of divine wisdom and don't be a copycat. Or a parrot—one who mindlessly echoes what others say. Create your own phrases that those other repeating rifles can fire off, repeatedly.

This is why simpletons love slogans.

They don't have to think.

Or create.

*How*ever, there are exceptions to the rule. A title can employ a cliché and therefore be easily remembered.

For example, my novel *Horse Thief.*

So groom your writing as you'd curry-comb your horse. If trying to sell a mare, would you take her to a horse fair covered with mud and her tail rife with burrs? No. Nor would you submit an ungroomed manuscript to an editor—or to your teacher.

Naturally there are deviations from our anti-cliché rule. And one of them is—you can create a character, some boring old cousin or uncle, who constantly utters (or rather parrots) one cliché after another. Instead of Monopoly, he plays Monotony, which is his only bored game.

Warning: Don't overdue his chatter. Because not quite enough is usually the right (write) amount.

About now, you just might be asking this question: Does boring, old know-it-all Robert Newton Peck ever include a cliché in his text narratives? Answer: Of course not.

I avoid them like the plague.

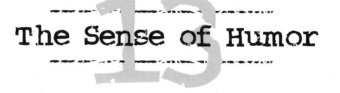

The Sense of Humor

Laughter.

If there's nothing funny in a book, I don't want to read it. Even a serious, dramatic novel needs to be lightened.

Ask a cook. Would your mother put a five-pound roast in the oven without first adding an herb or a spice? Not that I'm a gourmet. Truth is, I'm a contemptible cook. My cooking is so noxious that jungle natives dip their arrows in it.

Now then, before attempting to create humor, you first have to understand how it is *constructed*. Like a house, a boat, or a human skeleton, a joke has a basic structure. And it is a pig-simple blueprint to follow.

Humor is merely a bridge.

It's a connection, a sudden and unexpected span that unites two previously disassociated entities. A joke is that surprising arc-jump of light that flashes between anode and cathode. Comedy is a marriage of two objects, two ideas, two beings that were never before linked together.

Neil Simon was right.

Hilarity is *The Odd Couple*...a play about two once-married men whose wives had kicked them out the door. Ah, but for two opposite reasons! Felix is too neat, too tidy. Oscar is a messy disorganized slob. Now, because no one else can stand them, these two men share an apartment.

Comedy is the unexpected action that abruptly occurs in a common, everyday situation: "When I was born I was so ugly that the doctor slapped my mother."

Small wonder that Mom always hated me. And was always parking my baby carriage in a tow-away zone.

Learn to unite two elements that seemingly have no relation whatsoever. Human sexuality and a bug. There's no obvious association at all, is there? Until the humorist creates one by building a simple bridge to connect the pair: "No," said the female centipede crossing her legs. "A hundred times no."

Warning: Please resist getting a laugh at the expense of someone else's pain.

And never write a book or story to get even with an enemy. Laugh with people but never at them.

In *Horse Thief*, enjoy the conversationing between Hitch, an aging professional horse thief and his lifelong crony, Leroy.

> "Say, I disrecall, what was the year you'n
> me drove cattle for that Pan Handle outfit?"
> "It was 1903. Or half a hour later."

"That greedy town marshal took after us for sporting his wife. So we said if he'd forgive the charges, we'd allow him to ride herd all night. And keep every calf that dropped."

"Yeah, and by next morning, not even one calf got born, because the entire herd was all steers."

"The last laugh was on you. But I can't remember why you got tossed into the Gnawhouse jail. What did you do?"

"Well," said Hitch, "seems like I fell into financial disfavor, due to my investing funds on fast women and slow horses. The lady judge was a schoolmarm, and she insisted that my report card flunked me a F...in penmanship class."

Leroy raised a eyebrow. "Penmanship?"

"Yup. My pen wrote a bad check."

Knowing what humor is, its uses, and how it is so easily constructed will brighten your books. And your life.

A sense of humor makes sense.

Hey!

It's show time.

The theater curtain is rising, and you're the master of ceremonies, about to entertain an audience with a series of a dozen on-stage routines. Unfortunately, you made a major mistake. Every one of your acts features a trick bicycle rider.

A variety show without variety.

A fizzle.

A flop.

Your fiction will also take a painful pratfall unless you season your story by *pace*. Years ago, when I wrote my very first novel, I sort of stumbled into *pace* in *A Day No Pigs Would Die*. The first chapter is violent. Fast action, fear, and a plenty of pain. A boy (me) assists a troubled cow to rid herself of a half-born calf, a bloody and brutal birth that seriously injures him. This initial chapter ends as the lad's agony continues.

Chapter two in *A Day No Pigs Would Die* is the antithesis, a gentle and healing scene. At home. Several adults are tending this broken boy who's lying on a kitchen table. The entire atmosphere is now nesty and nurturing. One might conclude these two chapters are vastly different yet somehow blend.

Hit with a first chapter.

Heal with a second.

At the time, 1971, I knew almost nothing about arranging the elements, the events, in this true boyhood story. Quite by accident, this hit-and-heal combination luckily worked. Chapter two offered a quietude of relief to the reader, who, having endured the merciless mayhem of chapter one, welcomed a breather.

Here below is an example of a change of pace taken from the "Dear Elliot" chapter in my autobiography, *Weeds in Bloom*. My closest Army buddy was a Bronx boy who received amusing letters from his mother. Knowing that my own mother was illiterate and wouldn't be writing, Elliot shared his mom's letters with me.

> *Dear Elliot . . .*
> *Don't touch any guns. Unless you plan to grow up and become a criminal. Be sure to eat. If you're hungry at night, remind the sergeant that I'm a tax-payer and he should fix you a snack.*

> Elliot's right cheek was bruised and discolored from the mule-kick recoil of his M1 Garand weapon. His feet were swollen from marching, soft pinky hands blistered by heat and close-order drill, his body

purpled by bayonet practice. Butt strokes.
He took it on the chin.

Dear Elliot . . .
Be sure to get to bed early, and sleep
late. Are you taking the vitamins I sent you?
Do not get your feet wet. Who is this Rob
person you mentioned in your letter, the one
who hunted back home and knows guns? He
sounds like a gangster.

Due to being continually cold (and a
constant shortage of dry socks) our feet
tended to turn blue, then black and crusty
hard. With little or no feeling. It's called
trench foot. I held Elliot in my arms as a
medic, with forceps, took off one of his toes.

Dear Elliot . . .
Pray God you receive this box of
medicine. All kinds. You know your asthma
condition, so try not to inhale any foreign
air. At least here in New York we can see
what's to breathe. If in doubt, take two of
every pill I've enclosed.

In Italy, the mountains are steep,
especially when foggy and wet. Machine
guns and mortars weigh more than rifles.
A weapons platoon becomes no more than
mules.

Dear Elliot . . .
Don't carry anything heavy. Hernia runs
in our family, and your Uncle Isadore wore a
truss, we later discovered. And for years we
thought that dancing made him romantic.

In case you're not too savvy when it comes to music appreciation, ask a musical buddy of yours about a symphony's use of *pace*. Sometimes an opus bangs and booms by baritones and kettle drums. Then the composer throttles down by using strings, a violin, viola, and a cello. Softer still with a flute and piccolo. Haunting strains of double reeds, an oboe, or a lower-pitch bassoon.

Our auditory guard is down, and then we hear a sudden blare of trumpets, trombones, and those aristocratic fox-hunting horns with their flaring bells like a giant's golden lily.

We would all agree that a two-hour symphony of nothing but tuba honks might be overbearing to the point of madness.

Readers, as well as listeners, crave variety.

In your action, a change of *pace*.

Hit and heal.

Bathroom Bonus

Go!

Right this minute, drop whatever you're doing and hurry to your bathroom. Unless of course you're already *in* the bathtub reading this book.

Okay, in your bath chamber please yank all of the tissue from the roller, every square, and then closely observe the thing that's left on the spool. Big deal, you are possibly thinking, because it's merely a little, gray, four-inch-long core of cardboard, a cylinder that is inside every roll of toilet paper. And to think how many of these tiny tubes you have thoughtlessly discarded. Into a wastebasket.

For shame!

Today, save one. Give it a name, but be certain it's a name that suits its personality. Even more importantly, its potential, as this little core is a vital tool to a writer.

Let's call it Rooty-Toot.

Why?

Because on New Year's Eve, you'll take it to a party, and precisely at twelve o'clock midnight, raise it to your mouth, and through it, at the top of your lungs, you holler: "Rooty-Toot. Rooty-Toot. Rooty-Toot."

Don't be disheartened if your hosts presume that you've gone completely goo-goo, summon the police, and have you hauled away to the slammer. Cheer up. Once you've adjusted to the cozy comforts of a padded prison cell, you can examine your little gray cylinder and realize what a major contribution it shall be to your writing.

You see, these untalented dweebs who *don't* own a Rooty-Toot will still be writing unpublishable sentences such as . . .

"On Sunday, I took a stroll across a meadow and through a forest and saw many interesting things."

But not you. Because, as a proud and practical Rooty-Toot owner, you'll be raising it up to your *eye* (instead of your mouth) and *looking* through it. Result? Instead of writing a gosh-awful generality as did the dweeb above, you'll zero in. Concentrate on detail. Showing a reader how a tiny orange bug is walking along the vein of a leaf. And like all other living things, this bug knows where he's going. And why. He might even smile or glance up at you in anticipation, ecstatic that he might appear in a published book.

He might be thinking, "A star is born."

People who generalize and refuse to zero in tight on specifics won't succeed as authors. They merely announce that a bird flew by, too lazy to explain whether it was a two-inch, ruby-throated hummingbird or a giant California condor with a ten-foot wingspan.

You, on the other hand, might describe a flicker woodpecker, and we readers hear its fluttery trill or notice its white tail light as it flies away.

Or describe a bird as I did through the eyes of Henry Old Panther in *Nine Man Tree*:

> Ahead, an egret landed on a half-submerged log, folded her wings, then lifted a leg and balanced upon the other; a single stem of a white-feathered lily.
> 'I will not disturb you, my bird friend,' Henry silently told the egret, 'for it was perhaps your grandmother's grandmother who taught me how to wait with serenity.'
> Squinting in the misty gray evening, he rested his pole, now content merely to drift, observe. The egret stood motionless until a frog made a fatal move. Poking his head above the dark surface, close to a cypress knee, the bullfrog created a ripple.
> As its ring enlarged, Henry noticed.
> So did the white egret.
> It took three long breaths of time for the bird's free leg to unflex, extend, and finally touch the water one step closer to the frog. The rear leg, in no greater haste, did likewise. Then five unhurried steps, as though the feathered one knew no hunger. Without warning, her curved neck abruptly straightened into a long white lance; a yellow rapier of a beak spiked into the bullfrog, hoisting him high. Struggling,

legs kicking silvery beads of water, he almost instantly disappeared to become a squirming bulge in her gullet.

Because of your looking through a Rooty-Toot, we readers share minute miracles with you. How a female short-tail shrew, two inches long, is now in labor. From the strain, tiny beads of sweat appear on her rapier snout as her young are born, one by one, as blind and helpless, little pink gems of life. So wee that a hundred of them would weigh less than an ounce.

Now you have become an author.

A shrew has tamed you.

Important: Do not simply read this chapter and sort of promise yourself that you'll perhaps consider following my sage advice and never generalize. That's not professional.

If you be wise, you'll do this . . .

Keep your Rooty-Toot on your desk, at a place where you perform the arduous and ambitious chores of authorhood. Not lying down. No, your Rooty-Toot must be standing tall, a full four inches of able assistant, and ready to serve.

Look through it!

Zero in.

Tightrope

You won't need a rope.

A short length of ordinary string will do the trick.
Tie an end to something stable. Pull it taut. No slack.
Secure the opposite end so your string tightens to a
rigid, horizontal line.

Dare I say straight as a string?

Next step, imagine your hand is a circus performer.
Using your index and long middle finger as legs, two
fingertips as feet, start walking across your string
like a tightrope artist, being careful not to tumble.

This is how a good writer writes.

On a tightrope.

Aloft on a high wire, a tightroper always moves
straight ahead, toward a goal, which is the other end
of the rope. The finish. As he reaches it, the circus
band blasts a brassy *ta-dahhh* and everyone cheers.
However, had he taken a false step to either left or
right, what happens? He falls. As a writer, he fails.

Now for some fun and frolic. Here is how our amateur
author, Elmer Emerging, would perform *his* circus act:

It was midnight. Our wealthy,
expensively-dressed, and spoiled-rotten
heroine, Taffeta De Benture Dow-Jones, was
alone, unarmed, hurriedly walking along
a dark, dirty, deserted street in a high-
crime section of a city. Hearing heavy male
footsteps behind her, closer and closer, she
ducked into a convenient telephone booth.

Ah, but as she closed the door, a faint
overhead light clicked on, revealing that
Taffeta was no longer alone. The stranger was
large, hairy, and lecherously leering at her.

A naked gorilla!

Taffeta flinched. A gasp escaped her
lips. She couldn't resist smiling because
such a familiar situation rekindled
fond memories of her suburban Boston
hometown, Buzzard's Cud, and her
childhood. When not nestled in the posh
comforts of a parental homestead, Taffeta
spent many a pleasant hour next door with
Aunt Mildew, an eccentric who earlier had
tried to collect stamps. However, as nobody
ever wrote to her, Aunt Mildew plunged
into an alternative hobby.

Collecting telephone booths.

So prevalent, and easily obtained.

Night in and night out, Taffeta and
her aunt stalked many a darkened street
or alley, spotting a phone booth, using
crowbars to dislodge it, loading it onto
a pickup truck, and hauling it home.
Customarily this caper went smoothly. Not
always. Whenever there had been a person
inside the booth, trying to complete a call,
harsh words were heatedly exchanged.

For Taffeta, there were other nostalgic
recollections of youth and later, of a

ripening and blossoming maidenhood.

Her deepest secret.

At times when Aunt Mildew left to attend an embroidery circle or her kickboxing class, Taffeta began to visit their vast assembly of telephone booths. Checking every coin return cup in hopes of an unclaimed quarter. Adopting each and every stray animal that resided in booth upon booth. Giving them names.

For example, a thirty-foot python she called Muffin.

Does this inane chapter have a purpose? Yes. And here it be in a nutshell:

Do not be an Elmer. Whenever your Taffeta is cornered by a massive and menacing gorilla, stay with the story. The *here-now*. What's happening here and what's happening now. Resist wandering off to somewhere such as Buzzard's Cud and exposing your poor reader to pointless paragraphs of background mush. Stay in the telephone booth. Your story must move straight ahead like our high-altitude circus performer on a tightrope: toward a goal.

Keep to the high wire.

Don't go haywire.

Violets and Violence

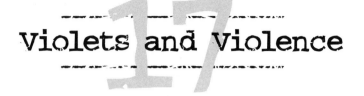

Happens every December.

A well-meaning friend mails me a Christmas card (for which I am truly grateful to receive) featuring a vast assortment of animals, resting, as though at a social event. The lion is lying down with a lamb.

Yes, it's a precious picture. But such an abnormality exists in Mr. Hallmark's mind. It surely ain't in Mother Nature's. In our real world the lamb is inside the lion.

Digesting.

Nature provides us with a bipartite planet. Half beauty and half brutality. Violets and violence. We humans are born selfish and brutal. In that order. A newborn baby thinks of no one but itself, its comfort, discomfort, or its hunger. In only a few years, it becomes brutal. Visit a playground and observe how unsupervised children can be physically brutal to one another.

If we eventually mature into merciful and sharing adults, it's due to a plenty of patient nurturing that our parents, teachers, and ministers bestow upon us.

We country folks call it *good raising*.

For decades, as an author, my living has been earned by combining violets and violence in every book. A poem and a punch. Some of the most entertaining motion pictures are comedy crime. Lighthearted larceny.

For an example of blending comedy into a crime, read *Horse Thief.*

As an author, you'll be more apt to succeed if you avoid writing about what people *ought to do*; and show *how*, in fact, they *really behave*. If all your novel's characters act like saints, you'll have editors, reviewers, and readers yawning a ho-hum. Somebody's got to play the hissed-at heavy. The villain. Bless his heart—because without Bruno Bully, you have no drama. No conflict. No tug.

Ask yourself this. How successful would *Bro*, the story of a boy who risks his life breaking the law to be with his newly-orphaned kid brother, be had I not included the sadistic prison-camp warden, Ogre O'Grady?

In short, bury a bit of barbed wire in your birthday cake. Among roses, insert a thorn. But be sure to explain *why* your villain is mean and the details that motivate his meanery. Branch Dockery's savagery in *Bro* is only meaningful when you learn the reason behind his madness.

Warning: It's in poor taste to shoehorn bits of violence into your story merely to attract attention.

Use a violent act only if it moves the story forward. Don't let a brutal scene be an uncomfortable pebble in a reader's boot.

Years ago, a very close buddy and I had considered writing a book together. He was a fine friend who served as best man when I got married. You already know him, on TV. Mister Rogers. To me, just plain, good ol' Fred. We couldn't agree on a premise, a core for our book, mainly because Fred was one side only of Mother Nature's coin. I'm the other. He was purely the nonviolent violet.

Although an ardent vegetarian, believe it or not, this kind and gentle gentleman deeply appreciated my bloody and brutal books of butchery. Perhaps he saw a violet in my secret soul that few others see.

Speaking of eats . . .

This is a true vignette: At a reception, a crowd of us stood at a long table that offered a feast of food. All kinds. Two college professors were there, stuffing their gaping maws with ham, beef, chicken, shrimp, and crab. All animal flesh. Between mouthfuls, they were discussing my earthy novel, *A Day No Pigs Would Die*, not sounding at all praiseful.

"Well," said one prof, "I'm always opposed to violence."

"Indeed," agreed the other, chewing, "As am I."

My dear father, Haven Peck, had killed hogs for a

living. How I wish he could have overheard their remarks. Papa didn't smile every year.

Yet right then he just might have.

P. S.—Believe it or not, I have dedicated two of my books to two of my deeply-appreciated college profs.

Mental Meanderings

Algebra.

As a high school freshperson, my incompletely-formed mind questioned the value of factoring algebraic equations. For me, math was a mystery. Oddly, the student who sat beside me, John Napier, seemed not befuddled at all.

In later years, I began to realize one of algebra's purposes—to exercise our intelligence. To churn our gray matter into areas that offered more depth than the lyrics of "*I Got the Boogie-Woogie Blues for Snooky Poo.*"

Pardon the cliché, but practice makes perfect. This is why vocalists sing la-la-la-la-la scales and boot-camp soldiers fire rifles at targets. This truism can also apply to writers. Especially emerging ones.

Like you.

In tennis, power stems from form, and form is a result of *practice*. Ditto for powerful piano playing. Practice! Therefore, release the vividness of your imagination. Let it holler. Run wild into meaningless exercises of irrational frivolity. Keep your exercise short and crisp. The shorter a poem or story, the more perfect it must be.

Lice
Adam had 'em

or

A very fast Honda
Ran over Jane Fonda.

A superb exercise to hone your funny bone is creating paragraphs that almost immediately close to a climax. A punch line. To guide your endeavors in this jocular jungle, here below are a few gobs and blobs that I, in carefree moments of abandon, managed to smirkingly scribble:

1. The mission's taco bells seldom bing-bonged in the quaint little Mexicano chapel, yet Padre Dom Perignon knelt once again to pray to the Blue Nun as he so (get it?) habitually did, imploring that Saint Pauligirl would make a holy visitation, perform a miracle, and convert his humble cask of Snapple into Cold Duck.

2. That night at Niagara Falls, the sound of thunderous megatons of water pounded without cease, invading our honeymoon suite with a relentless river of roar. Leaping out of bed, I stumbled into our bathroom and groped the toilet tank. To jiggle the handle.

3. *Oui.* She knew she was French, yet petite S'Oui DeBrie cringed whenever she was outside the farmhouse and heard her mother's insistent call,

summoning her to supper. Repeating, repeating, repeating her name: "S'Oui. S'Oui. S'Oui." Obediently, she always came into the kitchen. So did all of their pigs.

4. The fiery dents from his bucktoothed kisses still hissed and smoldered on her bruised and battered neck, causing Pandora to question her wisdom. *Why* had she opened Count Dracula's box? She presumed where he had learned and mastered the art of bloodsucking. Law school.

5. Alas, I was a fatherless boy. No one to take me fishing or to baseball games. I had nobody to call *Dad*, having been conceived in a laboratory as a test-tube baby. So, with a sigh on Father's Day, I gift-wrapped an Armani necktie and mailed it to a syringe at the We-Kid-U-Quick Fertility Clinic.

The above lumps of lunacy may strike you as idiotic. But trust me. This exercise of composing mental meanderings is both fun and fruitful. So create your own, or use any method to jostle loose your thinking in the mundane. From commonplace to comic.

It is the *unusual* that editors desire. And readers dig.

Go meander.

Ugly Poetry

Miss Kelly shared it with us.

At her modest one-room school on a Vermont dirt road, she was our only teacher for six years. We were the sons and daughters of millworkers, lumberjacks, farmers, and hog butchers. Very few of our parents could read or write.

In September, on the first day of school, we all arrived barefoot. From the ankles up, however, most of us had been scrubbed harder than a workshirt on a Monday morn washboard.

Every day she read us poetry.

How clearly I remember Miss Kelly informing us that a poem is a song you *say* instead of sing. With wording so pretty that it needs no music. On her desk there sat two boxes. One said "Pencils." The other? "Pencils too short to save." In our homes, items such as pencils and paper didn't exist, so our teacher supplied us with two sheets of white paper and a too-short pencil.

We were assigned the impossible.

Compose a poem.

I wrote mine about some kittens that were born in our barn, a wondrous miracle that blessed us every spring, and this poem earned my first gold star.

And eventually earned my living.

Hold on. Don't believe even for a breath that, generally speaking, a writer can earn a lush living by poetry. No way. Yet indirectly he can! *Poems are the push-ups of prose.* Sinewy sentences are strengthened by poetry's musical muscle. Get this straight and stick it in your craw: Poetry isn't confined to butterflies and buttercups. One can write poetically about an extremely ugly article. Ugly! Example: Dirty underwear.

At the start of chapter twenty-three in *Millie's Boy*, you'll find the following paragraph:

> It was late. The bunkhouse was dark and
> I felt my way along a row of snoring men
> to an empty cot. At first, I thought it was
> occupied as some lumberjack had hung his
> long underwear over the high footboard. To
> dry. The underwear was damp and didn't
> smell too clean. It just hung there, arms
> down on one side and legs down on the
> other, as tired as the man who'd soaped it.

Primordial (unprim) though it may sound, it's a chunk of writing I'm proud to claim—finding beauty where it is least expected. For you, perhaps it might occur on a rural road. You're passing a farmhouse, and there's a majestic shade oak, a frayed rope, and an old, wore-out, black tire hanging down. Silent and still.

In *My Vermont II*, you'll find the following poem:

Tire Swing

It took a toss or two, as I recall,
To throw a rope beyond a limb. A fling
Prodigious, so the rope would then descend
To knot around a tire for a swing.

It hung. A knot above, a child beneath
Kicking dusty feet in to-and-fro,
Amusing audience of oaken leaves,
Green hands in breeze, applauding for a show.

When I would swing, my cousin Ben would push
'Til he'd no longer reach my high return.
Or perhaps we'd shinny up the rope
To touch the giant's arm. Our hands would burn.

In later years, I'd sometimes walk a road
To pass a farm, where I could look and see
An empty tire on a fraying rope,
All underneath an emerald canopy.

A memory would often make me stop,
Seeing not a child within a hole.
Imagination then would we install
Myself inside, to fill the tire's soul.

Again I hear Ben Peck's cascading laugh,
Giggling his rubber-circled joy.
Or twisting round and round, until green world
Was spinning too. An oak tree's yo-yo toy.

My hands again feel black. Because a swing
Can spin a magic web so wondrous wild,
So silvery, so gold. It's sad to see
A hanging tire longing for a child.

Open Pages

Okay, you're living in a house.

Your south wall is almost entirely transparent glass because it's a very large picture window. Now comes an easy choice of two possibilities.

What manner of view do you prefer? Number one, a massive brick wall that is only inches outside your window, and all you're able to see is merely a ton of bricks? Number two, your other choice, a wide-open-space view, a panorama of a green and grassy meadow, dotted with mares and foals grazing in clover?

Number two is my pick of view, and I'll wager it certainly shall be yours.

Now picture a page in a book. And this hideous page is all one paragraph, an entire block of black type. Words, words, words—and, except for four margins, no white space. No fresh air.

No open vista. No oasis.

To your eye or mine, such an overcrowded page is unattractive, too hostile. Outside of your front door, would you place a mat that says "Scram," or do you prefer a friendly "Welcome"? The closed-up-tight, brick-wall page is saying "Scram" to the reader's eye, even before he comprehends the first word.

It's just plain uninviting.

Which of these is more inviting?

SCRAM!

A;lsdkjf;alksdjf;lkajsd;lkfja;lsk
djf;aoijwe;roikajhspd;voija;wp
erapoiwej;piajgipoajwe;ijfai alk
ej;foaijp;aijwe;oikjaf;ipogjaoikj
a;lkeijr;paoiujg'iapokje;ipfja;w
eiporja[p;ekjfa;oiweruj;oaikjf;a
poiweuj;ofija;oiweurj;aoikjf;alik
sjedfd;flkja;weoiru;aoijes;oriaoi
fjpoe;ijraoiwkejr;oaijecikj;oaijr;
oaiejf;oiakje;roija;eopirja;oiejr;
aoiejrf;oaiwejr;apoiejfoaiewjroi
awejr;o894upwo48u5o48iutols
idlri58u4potsiurej;soleioutjoas
iel4rutjlosierujtoislreuhjt;oairjt
;aoif;aoi4weruao;iguj;loakjeo[i
ajnva[ioengqoiwunvvoirutoire
ujt;oiserutpoiuoriu'goijs;poreu
soirut;oisut;oisruj;otijusoirujt;
oisjgosijr;toisjg;oipsrotijs;'oitj;r
oij;oisj;oihosijrt;spioj;oij;oijs;oij
re;osieutjaipjhoiaua'ojrt;'so;ori
gs;oijrt;soigj;soikrth;soihyuj'ao

COME ON IN!

She hit me.

"Ouch."

"Sorry. Did it hurt?"

"Sort of."

I liked Norma Jean so it was sort of all in fun, if you know what I mean.

Girls.

A mystery to me.

For years, I thought they were merely soft boys. But then I matured . . .

Well, you can guess.

"Rob?"

"I'm here."

"Sorry."

"Oh, it's okay."

"Like let's go get ice creams."

"Hey, that sounds cool."

Go back in time. Remember when you were a kid, marched to the school library, and once there you were commanded to select a book to read. Betcha did what I did. I flipped through a book really fast to take a preview squint at a lot of the inside pages. If they were overloaded and saturated by words, like a big brick wall, I rejected the book to choose one that looked open. Easier to read. Hospitable.

A plenty of wide, open spaces.

Like a meadow.

Oh, another very important thought on how a page ought to *appear* prior to its being *read*. And that's this: How should a paragraph *look*? Well, I'll share with you what always works for me.

To begin with, avoid making your paragraphs the same length. That's boring. Some can be short. Others long.

Avoid the usual declarative sentence, and begin it with a dependent phrase. "Leaning on a fence post, Pa lit a pipe, and then spoke about our oxen." This will add variety to your style.

Within a single paragraph, and let's examine a large one, *alter the length of your sentences*. A good idea is to occasionally toss in a sentence of two words, or even one. Try it. See? *Variety*, once again, persists in being our motto, playing a key role in the artistic, physical beauty of a paragraph or a page.

Do I practice what I preach?

Test me. Study the structure of these single pages from *Cowboy Ghost* and *Horse Thief*. And, while you're at it, be persnickety enough to take a closer examination of one of my longer paragraphs.

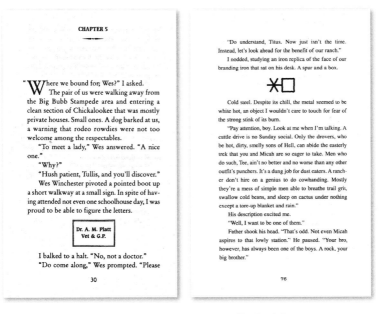

Now when you're writing *your* stuff, do likewise. Copycat my style.

It ain't merely a page you're presenting.

A page is more than a sheet of paper.

It's a visual variety show.

An invitation!

Research

A cow.

How long since you've touched one?

A week? A year? Maybe a decade. Golly, I certainly dread to think that you have never touched a cow in your entire life. Where do you live, in a closet?

Whoa! Let's take a different tack. How long since you stood yourself beside a horse, a mare, gently picked up her hoof and held it between your knees? Feel it. Use a thumbnail to flick off a bit of grit. You'll discover that her hoof is soft. Not hard.

Do you ever crawl under a car? Or open a baseball, golf ball, or a telephone—just because you're curious to learn the secrets that lie inside?

Research is far more physical than intellectual. It is the solid *stuff* that makes a novel ring rich as a church bell. Genuine research is not checking statistics or demographics in a library. It's forcing yourself off pavement, following a gravel road, meeting and knowing plain people who earn an honest living by soiling their hands.

More importantly, getting *your hands* dirty.

Try it. Plant a seed. Feel it cleanse your soul.

The successful author regards himself as a manufacturing plant. A factory that imports raw materials to build something that'll sell to somebody. However, nobody will buy it unless the author (our plant foreman) manages to round up quality stuff, then hammer it into a shape that performs a job. A function.

Its work is to entertain. To inform, or perhaps merely to amuse.

Rather than being an artist, I am a builder. Robert Newton Peck, construction worker. Ah, but no matter how cleverly I work my tools, what I construct will be a flop unless I first do what? Answer: Hunt and gather.

Gather raw material. In this trio of words, only one is paramount in its importance. Can you guess which of the three is key? Give up? All right, I'll tell you.

Raw!

By raw, I mean unrefined. In its natural state. Wild and wooly. Untamed. Uneducated. Unpolished. Hunks of iron ore that you, a hardworking craftsman, can smelt, mold, pound, file, and forge into an artistic article.

Is writing an art or a craft?

Don't get uppity.

Best you make yourself cocksure of which is which.

Rob gathering raw material in the form of a giant boar hog for *Nine Man Tree.*

You are the craftsman, a millworker with dirty hands. But what you deftly manufacture is art.

Ever see a woodchipper? Feed twigs and branches into its open bin. In seconds, the blades reduce them to mulch. So chopped up that it's near to being dust. Think of yourself as a woodchipper. The pivotal term is *feed*. Meaning what? Well, it necessitates your constant search for more and more raw material to be *fed* into your head. A hungry hopper.

Make it a habit to observe every repair guy who comes to your house to fix or adjust some mechanical gizmo. Learn its parts. Their function. Familiarize yourself with the tools that assemble them. Ask questions! Take a course in *repair* and become handy with your hands. Discover the different types of hammers, saws, and wrenches.

Study hardware at a hardware store.

Pester your school's music director, Mr. Pralltriller, to show you every instrument in the band and orchestra. Befriend a classmate who plays a bassoon or the mellophone and inquire how each works. Learn to play some kind of musical geegaw yourself. In fact, make a habit of learning from every person you meet!

Visit every kind of mill or factory in your county!!!

Years ago, at a giant New York City corporation, I was vice president of advertising. In charge of producing radio and TV commercials, jingles, and print ads. Big corner office to befit my big important title. Yet on my wall there hung a tiny little framed motto of just six humble words.

*I make things
that sell stuff.*

Hey, as an author, that's sort of your mission—to make things that sell. To do such, better begin with the highest-quality *raw* material you can locate. Off pavement. In the wild. Remember that this chore is more search than research. More hunt than gather. The goal is to stuff yourself full of *stuff.*

You might find yourself a cow. If so, go touch her.

Thirst.

One evening it got a grip on you. Result? You gulped a gallon of iced tea, downed a couple of quarts of lemonade, a cola six-pack, plus a liter of root beer. No longer thirsty, you went straight to bed.

Needless to say, in the middle of the night, you really had to go somewhere. Nature didn't just call. She was hollering for help. So you stumbled around in the inky darkness, hurriedly en route to relief.

"Ouch!"

Instead of a john, your foot found a thumbtack. A merciless pricker is embedded in the center of your right heel. You certainly weren't out of bed to search for a thumbtack. Yet there it was. Surprise! Whenever this happens, not often, you are a lucky author. It happened to me. Prior to getting my very first book accepted by a publisher, I had made myself a long list of possible titles:

Hard Work   *Life on a Dirt Road*
Uphill Family   *A Boy and a Dad*
My Father and Me   *Pinky*
Five Acres   *Hard Scrabble*
My Pig   *My Pet Pig*

None of them seemed to click. Not a one was inspiring. As the list grew, the duller they all became. Finally. The thumbtack! I had absolutely no idea that a sentence that I'd already written in the last chapter would be my most famous title, awkward as it is, until I looked down at a page. And lo! There it was, staring up at me. A simple sentence.

"A day no pigs would die."

Enough said.

Titles are important, so give them a plenty of thought. Make a list and keep making it until a thumbtack fangs your foot. The time will be wisely spent. And here's why.

For every person that reads your book, there will be a thousand that will only read the title. Let's hope they'll remember it and possibly remark to a friend, "Ah, I've heard of that book or its author, Elmer Emerging." At parties, some may falsely claim they've read it.

Title droppers.

Decades and decades ago, when I was a knee-high sprout, Papa and I were repairing a roadside rail fence. A young neighbor, Jeb Furman, braked his pickup, dismounted, and started swapping lies with my father. I only listened.

"Jeb, how many kids you'n Myrna got?"

"Pair. Boy and girl."

Haven Peck, my farmer father who could neither read nor write, seemed happy to hear it. "A boy and a girl," he repeated. "Jeb, that's a king's order."

I'm a mature man now. Well, maybe not mature but at least six-four, and a proud sire of a stout son Christopher and a darling daughter Anne. If I get around to writing a book that is strictly devoted to my two children, it shall be my father, Haven Peck, who titled it.

A King's Order.

Recently, in 2004, it was my honor to visit South Carolina's magnificent military academy, The Citadel. I wept there. Because I stood at attention by General Mark Clark's grave to give my overseas commander a final and respectful salute.

There's more.

Happened at the end of World War II when, on the Italy-Yugoslav border, I met Mark Clark. A mud-spattered jeep bounced into our area. Out stepped two senior officers. One appeared six and a half feet in height, a crowbar for a spine, plus a neat row of impressive stars on his steel helmet. The strap hung loose. His strong hatchet face could split kindling. A single word described him.

Soldier.

I had just turned eighteen and I'd never seen God

before, and there he stood, returning our salutes, approaching us. He admired his Eighty-Eighth Infantry and told us so. Close up, with his hand gently resting on my dirty olive-drab shoulder, he asked me a direct question.

"Where's home, son?"
I swallowed. "Vermont, Sir."
"Shot a few rabbits for your mom's cookpot?"
"Yessir. And I missed a few."
Leaving, he patted my shoulder.
"You'll do fine."

On that unforgettable day, our general was reviewing troops in the company of an aging, bandy-legged bird colonel. Two tired men burdened by battle. As they slowly moved away, I overheard the colonel ask, "General, were we ever that young?"

General Mark Clark answered with three words.

"Toys of war."

Someday, better be soon, I'm going to consider writing about my war. Each soldier has his own that nobody else knows of. My story won't cover all of Europe, or Italy, or our complete Eighty-Eighth Blue Devil Division. Only a few beardless baby boys who sometimes whispered "Mama" in the night and by dawn's dreary daylight tried to stand as men, keeping Yugoslavia out of Italy. How proud I am to have served at their sides.

I have already been blessed by a title.

Toys of War.

Sound Off

Do you ever watch television?

If you do, then you've probably heard a member of your family holler in your direction: "Please! Please turn down the *sound*."

Now, for your betterment, I'm going to act completely contrary to the member of your family whose eardrums are exploding.

Turn the sound *up*!

No, not on TV. That should be turned *off*. We're discussing how your own writing style will improve, and I mean *a lot*, when you start adding *sounds* into your story.

If it's morning on a farm, let your reader hear a rooster crow, a barn door open. The metallic music of a blacksmith shoeing a horse. Is Papa awake? I hear him cough, perhaps clumping big boots down wooden stairs. Outside, the clank of milk pails and the soft breathing of a Holstein cow. Hear a farmer's hand pat her flank? Perhaps speak to her in a gruff but gentle voice.

"Good morning, Bessie."

Once a bucket is beneath her udder, then straight
streams of milk begin to chime the pail in a steady
pulse. The waftings of work.

Do goats bleat? Sheep? Lambs? A hungry calf waiting
to mother-up. A tractor start. Out on a field, a shovel
is biting into topsoil or a plowshare swims its furrow.
As a farmer lays a leather harness to a Percheron's
broad back, let me hear the traces buckle and snap.
And then listen to Dobbin's snort. A big draft horse
will rap hoof iron to drum a barn's wooden floor.

It's evening.

Two boys lie on their backs on a brown bed of
pine needles, harkening to the moonlit bugle of
coonhounds. A Vermont mountain boy's ear can
read every bark.

Who lives next door?

Is it some untalented child who is being forced
to practice his violin? Mother insisted. Is Father
objecting? Saying a naughty word? Throwing
something. Does it break a window? If so, *let me
hear it.*

Who's coming along the walk? No need to get up
from the squeaking porch swing to look, because
Uncle Rafe walks with a limp and a cane. His left
shoe drags as he hobbles along, scratching the
sidewalk with every other step. His limp and its
noise are very much a part of Rafe's character.

Let's think music.

When, in human history, did it begin? I have a
theory. A single hairy hunter is waiting for game, to
kill fresh meat, and like all who wait, he is bored.
His thumb begins to strum the string of his weapon.
His bow. Nearby, a second hunter hears. Strums
his. The subtle sound is somehow pleasing to these
primitive people. And guess what?

A harp is born.

Centuries and centuries later, a shepherd boy sits
on a hillside, overseeing a flock of sheep. They are
grazing and he has little to do. Until he finds an arm-
long reed and blows through it. The sound is pretty
to his ear. Trouble is, the reed has a hole. Ah, if he
places a fingertip over the hole, the musical note
changes its pitch. He has a two-note melody.

What, he possibly wonders, if I punch more holes?
Use more fingertips? Create an entire scale of notes?

A flute is formed.

His elder brother, or father, is the bow-hunter
harpist, and they entertain the other cave people
by a duet. One cannot tune a simple reed flute, so
the hunter tunes his by tightening or loosening
the string of his bow. Perhaps this was the dawn of
harmony.

Warning: Not all sounds are charming. An alarm

clock. The car horn of an impatient motorist. And the worst of all, a crying baby. It's three o'clock in the morning, but to the baby it is *snack time!* Once he is changed and fed, the infant will silently sleep. Not before a mother hums a lullaby. She isn't a talented singer. Yet to anyone listening, old or young, her voice is worthy of a choir of angels.

Dad snores.

But I'm your *reader*, dear writer, and you'll be wise to let *me* hear. As well as listening to the orchestra of sounds, pleasant and unpleasant, that pepper your prose.

Lemme hear it.

Sound off.

More than a tune.

It's a haunting hymn.

Gracefully gliding through a novel there can sometimes spawn keynotes of a musical theme that subtly supports the story's premise. Its mysterious nourishment adds rhythm that throbs the heart.

Sometimes it has no name.

Yet it exists as a sparrow's highest melodic trill, towering above all other elements, bestowing the story a soul. Not all books have a theme song. Nor do all churches boast a steeple, a spire that thrusts straight upward where its tip tries to touch a cloud. Or its carillon cheers our ears.

Boy, I would be stumped to have to pinpoint, or hum, the theme of all sixty-five of my books. Some are songless. Yet when a novel composes one, I feel so rewarded, so uplifted.

For example, *Nine Man Tree* is a Florida swamp tale about a poor family whose name is Tharp. The father is little more than a sadistic sot. A drunkard. The mother is decent but helplessly trapped. She has two children. A small daughter with the Biblical

name of Havilah. Her slightly older brother is eleven
and he is Yoolee Tharp. The conflict, however, is the
awesome presence of a five-hundred-pound wild
hog. A big, mean tusker.

Now then, are any of the above beings the soul of
Nine Man Tree? No. Its soul is really a minor character.
Henry Old Panther is so old that he cannot remember
his age or even his family.

A hermit.

It is Henry who realizes that soon he will willingly
die. Alone, in order to join the Spirit Mother,
he must lie down, close his eyes and climb the
imaginary Nine Man Tree, a cypress taller than
all others. So massive as to require nine warriors
holding hands in a circle to reach around the base of
its gray majestic trunk.

Ah, but Henry Old Panther is not quite ready for
death just yet. A mission keeps him alive.

His secret purpose is to protect the pair of gold and
silver towheaded children from all harm. Yoolee and
Havilah are not aware that Henry is watching, on
guard. He stands so still that he is virtually invisible.

His song is green silence.

Poetic inevitability demands, of course, that at the
novel's conclusion the giant boar and aging Henry
Old Panther will meet. To die together.

Thus the story ends . . .

    High in the uppermost twigs and
delicate cypress lace of the Nine Man Tree,
a wren warbled her sweet song of welcome
and the muddy feet of Henry Old Panther
began an effortless climb into the clouds.
    Spirit Mother opened her arms.

Adult Language

What a lie!

What an outrageous lie.

Who tells it? The motion picture producers of
Hollywood and the television program producers
tell the American public (including our children) that
filthy language is grown-up talk.

It's how *adults* speak?

I'm no saint.

Were you to compile a list of all of *my* faults, my sins
and shortcomings, it might be longer than your leg.
However, there's one thing I resist doing, and that's
using a vile, four-letter epithet in any of my books.
And that includes a plenty that were written for *adults*.

Unfortunately, perhaps due to our staggering
numbers of overpopulation, we humans have
managed to soil our lovely planet Earth into a garbage
dump. Air unfit to breathe. Lakes and rivers unfit to
drink or swim in. Oceans so noxious that whales and
dolphins commit suicide by beaching themselves on
beaches, smeared and stained by oily tar.

All this, plus a lot of loud, tasteless noise.

Pollution is everywhere. Foul-mouthed rappers are constantly warping minds and morals as they air their electronic sewage. I can't stop it. No individual can. Yet you, as a writer, can help elevate our society above sludge. When you write, keep your story as clean as you can make it. If clever, you'll easily depict a dirty, rotten bum without lowering yourself to his standards.

Or his vocabulary.

For example, in this passage from *Bro*, Ogre O'Grady, warden of the Pecan County Correctional Camp, has just learned of Broda Joe Dockery's pardon, signed by Judge Singletary.

> Ogre had hisself a notion.
> As he kicked his office desk, the get-even idea slashed half a sour smile on his mouth, but there be no gladness in it. He'd just do smart and sneak around the cussed pardon.
> Dockery busted out. He would make Dockery pay. In blood.
> Problem be, his deputy wardens was all dumb bunnies. Nary a bit of brain in any of 'em. That's what make his plan so slick, because he'd pit jailbird against jailbird. There wunt be none of his deputies in on the collar.
> "I use my meanest cons. Or maybe   just one."
> He already know which of the convicts had poke sport at the Dockery boy, calling him Girlie Face. Well, now he'd give them baddies another crack at him.
> Wouldn't be death. No, it'd be ten time worse. After a while, poor Dockery wouldn't be human no more.

Just a cornered crazy animal.
"Dumb."
Ogre knowed he'd done a dumb-ass thing,
telling the chief of police that Dockery git away.
Simple to see that Percival Sweetbutter work
against him. Judge also against him. Weren't
fair, both of them peoples on Dockery's side
instead of his'n.
Using a con on this caper to nab Dockery, he'd
shift the blame on a prisoner, if matters go wrong.
Claim he break out. "Nobody escape Walter P.
O'Grady."

Plainly, the prison camp warden is nothing but crud.
And yet my novel *Bro* portrays him without using
his language.

If you're desperate to make someone notice you, attract
attention by standing naked on a restaurant table and
shouting filth. A few people may even crowd around
you and applaud. But ask yourself this: Are these the
persons you'd invite into your home or in your life?
Not in mine. There is nothing adult about dirty words.
I confess, when I was only nine or ten and knew no
better, using a crayon, I printed a few unpardonable
words over a boys' room urinal. I didn't know what a
lot of them meant. And the rest I misspelled.

Enough said.

Please remember—profanity is pollution. Honor your
audience. True adult language is clean and decent.
Words you'll teach *your* children.

Words that raise you up to authorhood.

Max and My Mom

Apple pie.

Always my favorite because my mother (No! Not yours. *Mine!*) baked the world's best. Due to the fact that Vermont's cold weather is exactly why a green pie-apple tree thrives.

A mile distant, I could inhale its fragrance. Mama pulled her apple pie from the kitchen stove oven and always set it on a window sill to cool. To settle. By suppertime, it was solidly ripe for carving. Any premature cutting would have ruined it too soupy to serve.

Why?

Why am I telling you about a pie?

Because of Mr. Max Schuster.

The year was 1962. A law school friend, Dave Goodstein, was hosting a dinner party in his posh Manhattan townhouse. Across the table sat a very diminutive gentleman who turned out to be none other than Dick Simon's partner. Together they were the ramrods of a very prestigious publishing entity.

Simon and Schuster.

Jumping up on him like a puppy with muddy paws, I eagerly blurted out that I wanted to become an author. Not yet published. Max groaned, rolling his eyes, dreading that I'd be pestering him with questions. And worse, threatening to describe an in-progress manuscript in full detail.

Reading his apprehensive expression, I flashed him my winning country-boy grin, requesting that he offer me just one smidgeon of advice. One? Please, just a helpful hint to forever follow. In a sense, his surprising response made me suspect that Mr. Max Schuster might have been kin to my mother. All he advised was a tidy gem of nine words:

"Write with fire. But cut with a cold knife."

Ever since that enlightening evening, I've followed his sage advice to the letter. After I write a chapter or two, with fire, I set it aside to cool. Later, usually the next day, I edit it, cut it, and prepare it to serve to a hungry editor.

Hey, it's worked for me.

Sixty-five times.

Oh, another useful tip, from me instead of from Max. Whenever you complete chapter six, don't up and quit for the day. Immediately begin chapter seven, even if it's merely a paragraph or two. Then, on the following day, you'll already hit the ground running. In motion. You'll avoid having to stare at a blank sheet of paper, headed by "Chapter Seven" and nothing beneath except the emptiness of writer's block.

To sum it all up . . . bake a pie, allow it to cool, and only then do you start to cut it. This wisdom comes to you with the courtesy of Mr. Max Schuster.

And my mom.

Get Grammarous

'Twas a sunny and summery Saturday afternoon on Long Island. There I lay, exhausted from volleyball, sprawled on a beach to await pigmentary alteration as Plethora slowly strolled by. Tan and tawny, her hips rolled to, fro, undulating so oceanically that I reach for my motion sickness pills.

Her bikini she could carry in a change purse.

How could I get to meet her?

I pursued. What red-blooded, American, glandular-intensive guy wouldn't paw dirt and then chase a gal like Plethora Biltmore? Lucky me. After only an hour of pleading, I managed to get her telephone number and also learn that she resided in a Manhattan apartment with three other supermodels. Sutton Place. How handy, as I lived in nearby Hell's Kitchen.

Needless to add, I gave her a call. After what seemed to be an eternity of seven rings, a female and flirtatiously feline voice purred a . . .

> "Hello."
> "I'm Rob Peck," I panted. "Are you Plethora?"
> "This is *her.*"

Unable to tolerate tearful good-byes, I hung up. For good reason. Because one of my hang-ups is somebody who uses improper grammar. *How* I longed to hear her whisper those three little words: "This is she." Based on the ironclad mandate that the verb to be demands (and practically cries out in the darkness for) a nominative case pronoun.

There's a moral to this tale.

Be aware of *how* you speak, in person or in print. Your manner of speaking is a key element in *how* high you'll escalate in society. Sound like a bum and you'll be treated as one. Your grammar deserves more grooming than your hair.

*How*ever, if your character is a rodeo bronc rider, named Cody Chapstick, improper grammar might be colorful. Even entertaining. On a higher plain, if she is Lady Affluentia Silverspoon, so patrician that it takes her a dozen bites to eat a grape, best you manicure her mouth as well as her fingernails.

"Me and her seen a movie pitcher," won't cut it.

"She and I seen a movie pitcher," is correct.

Returning to our subject and sanity . . .

Discipline your diction. It is every bit as important as *how* you *look*. Looks aren't everything. Here's proof. You own a TV set. If the picture is perfect but the sound is static, you'll junk it. Now listen. *You* are a TV set. You have *sound* as well as picture. Work on both. Try to talk like Diana Rigg instead of a vacant and gum-chewing Trixie Shebang.

Lose saying "like" and "you know."

Same for that tired term . . . "relationship."

Flush 'em.

Okay, let's say you're a teenage child (no, you aren't a young adult until you move out, work, support yourself, pay bills, and pay taxes). Because you have a cell phone, driver's license, and a fake ID, you may have falsely concluded that if you don't already know it, it's not worth knowing.

Wrong. You learn for a lifetime.

It's possible, ten years from now, that you'll write a novel. A good one. When you travel to New York City to meet an editor, best you don't sound like the Greek philosopher, Ignoramus, who said, "Grammar—you know, like who needs it?"

Start *now*.

Not a decade from now.

Get grammarous. As it truly is glamorous. Enticing. Alluring. The sooner you begin to groom your grammar, in speech and on paper, the higher you'll climb.

Not *everyone* gets to the top.

But *anyone* can.

Nearby.

Perhaps less than a mile from where you live, there's a public library. Enter. Go inside and I'll wager you won't believe what you'll find.

A *librarian!*

As you know (ho hum) I've written sixty-five books. Are they all different? Sort of. Yet they all have one thing in common. *A librarian helped me write every single one.*

There's not a computer in existence, now or ever, that can replace the personal sensitivity of a dedicated librarian.

Thank goodness that at every library, there's a guardian angel sitting at the reference desk. The librarian, let's call her Martha Anne, is bored and has absolutely nothing to do except put a foot up on her desk, to paint a toenail. On seeing me, however, she smiles a helpful smile, secretly knowing how inept I am. Especially in pinpointing the distinct difference between a pralltriller and an uninverted mordent. To be serious, when you're stuck in your book-writing mud, a librarian will hie to *your* rescue. Count on it. Librarians know *how.*

Years ago, when I lived in Connecticut, a yet
unpublished Robert Newton Peck was nothing
but a literary nobody. On a Saturday morning,
wandering through the impressive Ferguson Library
in Stamford, I couldn't locate what I sought and let
out a sad sigh. A senior librarian took me (lucky me!)
under her able wing and we found info on a capstan
crank's capacity to budge inch-by-inch a heavy
object. Using ox power. As a boy, Papa had used a
capstan, but the memory of it had faded.

This librarian's grandfather, long gone, had used
one. Together, we worked it out and even assembled
a makeshift model. It helped to add accuracy to
chapter four of *A Day No Pigs Would Die.* A year later,
I presented her with an early autographed copy to
show my appreciation.

She also assisted my checking a few facts for later
novels.

Librarians are your friends and helpmates.

Sex Novel

A hot, panting sex novel?

Well, try as I might, I'll never be able to write one.
I don't know *how*. An author must write about
what he knows, avoiding the activities at which
he is pathetically unskilled. Legions of ladies have
suggested that I stick to farming and ranching.

Pigs, horses, and cows.

In 1947, I met Sloan Wilson, who soon became the
author of *The Man in the Gray Flannel Suit* and *A
Summer Place*, plus a dozen other bestsellers. Sloan's
younger brother, Jeff, was a buddy my age, but Sloan
(eight years older) was my idol. He willingly gave me
advice and encouragement. Foolishly, I tried to copy
him, attempting novels about Wall Street bankers
and Philadelphia lawyers, their sophisticated peers
and environs—preppy and Ivy-educated. I couldn't
pull it off convincingly as characters of their ilk were
known to Sloan. Not to me. All of my early efforts
were turned down faster than a hotel bed that has a
tiny chocolate on its pillow.

It's tough to paint portraits of unmet people.
So, with a shrug and a sigh, I dedicated three weeks
of my yet unpublished life to telling my own brief
boyhood adventure, a Vermont farm and family. A

cinch to write as I had lived it all. This little novel just flowed as leisurely as an April brook through a cow pasture.

A Day No Pigs Would Die. Knopf published it in 1972 at $4.95 per hard copy. Today, this identical book sells for $25. It's read worldwide in many languages. Required reading all over the U.S.A.

Beginner's luck.

*How*ever (and here's where *you* come in), this novel was written by an expert. Me. Because I was an expert on knowing *my own life*, exactly as you vividly remember yours. Nobody knows *you* as well as you do. So hurry. Go look in a mirror, grin, and greet yourself.

"Hi! Pleased to meetcha. Wanna be in a book?"

An Ivory soap percentage (99.44 percent) of all successful first novels are truly autobiographic. An author writing about himself, his family, pets, *chores*, and home town. Or city block. Please note that I stress *chores* because the hard physical work that people do is so essential to establish characters, the girders of your story. We want your actions. *Not your feelings.*

Listen up.

If you've never resided at the North Pole, resist locating your novel there, a story about a crying Eskimo named Blubber . . .

The polar night lay blacker than
death. A wind whipped and the snow kept
snowing. Mercury dropped lower and
lower. Way below zero. The temperature
grew colder and colder. Suddenly hearing a
noise behind me, I froze.

Enough nonsense.

To be serious once again. Write about familiar
environment. As a young green seedling, let it
sprout upward from your own dirt. Stay put. *Home.*
Even if it's a shoddy, five-acre Vermont farm;
you're twelve, poor, and all you possess is a piglet
named Pinky.

Do what I did. Spin a short story of a puny place,
plain people, and events that affect few folk, yet
deeply matter to one individual.

You.

"I'd better drive. I'm too drunk to walk."

I detest New Year's Eve. It ought to be called Amateur Night because people who generally don't drink a drop get spit-faced. Loaded. A snoot full. And worse, try to steer a car.

Alas, I'm going to a New Year's Eve party.

Who's the host?

My dear pal, Elmer Emerging, who says he's having a band, hors d'oeuvres—and at midnight, a giant magnum of very expensive champagne. The party is weeks away, but Elmer impatiently keeps uncorking his big bottle of Perrier Jouët. Why? To allow me and several other buddies a preview of its bubbly bouquet.

Elmer does this several times. By the time New Year's Eve arrives, oops! The cork doesn't pop. There's something missing in the champagne. It's flat. What has it lost?

Fizz.

Here's your lesson to learn: When building a book, and you're abrim with enthusiasm, you'll be tempted to tell (or bore) people about it. So frequently that the novel loses its momentum. It's lifeless. Do not preview it prematurely. Not that others will steal it. Let it remain private and personal because it keeps you bubbling if your champagne stays corked. Tight. When it is finally published and in bookstores . . .

Pop!

In progress, resist sharing it even among members of your family. Don't even repeat a single sentence to Lickspittle, your cat, who is probably far more interested in your goldfish.

Keep your champagne bottled.

Fizz beats flat.

P. S.—However, there are often exceptions to rules. And here's one regarding fizz. If you're doing your writing in a classroom under teacher supervision, be willing to share what you have written with others, and be supportive of their work.

Stand Tall

Psst . . .

Can you keep a secret?

Here goes: One of the secrets of my success is knowing who my audience is and forging fiction for them. This is not sophisticated market research.

It's horse sense.

Be business as well as bard.

My readers are the Vanilla People of our society. Not overly spiced. Like me, a vast majority are just plain, friendly folks—and there are millions and millions of them. Where do they reside? Let's be guided by *facts.* According to postmarks on my fan mail, they live in small cities and even smaller towns, suburbs, rural ranching and farming communities that have bookstores as well as schools and libraries.

Their letters manifest both patriotism and reverence. I call them by a comfortable down-home name . . .

God Bless Americans.

They are the bowel and backbone of our great nation. Millions grew up reading my *Soup* books (fourteen in all) and now their children are hooked on the newer titles. I feel close to them.

As you read **HOW**, its author is seventy-eight.

I've learned this: Working as a professional and prolific writer is rooted and anchored in more than the obvious rewards.

Warning: If your ego and greed strive only for fame and fortune, your personal character will wilt and wither into meaningless mush. You'll have all the depth of a damp sidewalk. Fame and fortune are cosmetic facades. Shallow surface. Inside yourself, stand tall for the creeds your parents taught you, and believe in the traditions you hold in your heart.

Speak and write the solid substance of your mind. No one else's. But always continue to constantly evaluate your positions, and don't blindly conclude that you're one-hundred percent right and the other person is dead wrong.

Our nation needs as many diverse opinions as we have varying fingerprints. Ergo, the thrust of this chapter is to inspire *your* independence. *How* do you envision yourself? I hope not as a member of a group or bloc, but as a unique individual. On the front of your novel, you'll never have to state your faith, race, color, voting habit, or romantic preference.

There's just one name.

Yours.

Do your readers a favor. Stand tall.

You'd have respected my grandfather.

Newton Peck was a man of Vermont granite, a grower, logger, builder of Shaker furniture, unable to read or write. Yet he sang hymns without a hymnal, quoted Scripture, and engaged in what he called *moonlight farming.* That means he stilled whiskey. Many good people do. Allow my quickly adding that many good people do *not* and stand strongly against it. Bully for you.

> "Grandad," I once asked, "why do you make corn likker?"
> "Because," he said, "Montpelier claims I cannot." This stubborn stance was then punctuated by a fierce nod of a very independent American head. Grandad Peck had eyes like eagles.

So, when *you* write, stand up straight for your own individualism. Standing right behind you will be men like Newton Peck and his grandson.

Pranks

Elmer, lighten up.

Resist being *dead serious* in every chapter of your yawning tome. Why? Because to a reader, that's exactly what it is. Deadly. Dreary. Dismal.

Having already read *A Day No Pigs Would Die*, you are already aware that, at moments, this story is stone-cold reality. New England gray. Several deaths, plus a pile of poverty. Yet sprinkled upon its heft are sparkles of levity and laughter.

Life should not be leaden.

Brighten up.

As an emerging author, you might want to perk your prose with an impish prank. It may not further the plot, yet it definitely establishes a facet of a character's personality. The scorpion prank in *Cowboy Ghost* is a solid example of how a prank established not only characters but also a level of bunkhouse humor.

In the story, a new cowhand, Jilly, had unkindly treated the ranch's Chinese cook, Tin Pan, prompting the other hands to play a prank on Jilly. Because Tin was only one third Jilly's size and needed some intervening to even the odds.

It began at the workday's end.

Dust finally settled and so did supper.
Bug Eye was torturing his harmonica;
both coonhounds were fed and asleep.
Cleopatra yawned, arose, stretched, and
considered hunting for a slow mouse.

"Something's up down yonder," Mrs.
Krickitt announced to Micah and me,
tossing a pink-and-white checkered dish
towel over her shoulder. She looked beyond
her kitchen window. "Trouble brewing on
every griddle. I can smell it."

The odor arrived, in person, in the
familiar form of Vinegar Swinton, elder
statesman of the bunkhouse and frequent
program chairman of a few horizontal
refreshments (I don't mean billiards) at
The Bent Ace.

"Miz Krickitt," he said through the
screen door, holding a battered sweat-
stained hat in one hand while scratching
himself with the other, "some us waddies
got the internal infernals. Kink knots."
He almost blushed. "A misery of a
constipationary nature."

"I know," she sighed to Vinegar. "No need
to diagram it all out, or put it to poetry."

"The boys and me . . . well, we was kind
of wondering, amongst ourselves, if'n we
might pervert upon your good nature to let
us maybe borrow a bottle of that there Let
Loose mineral spirit."

Our housekeeper raised an eyebrow.
"Vinegar, I believe I'm commencing to
understand your particular request."
Shaking her head, she opened a cabinet
door. "Mineral oil?"

"Yes'm . . . if you please."

She handed him a nearly full bottle of the colorless liquid medication, known among the illiterate afflicted as Let Loose.

"Thanks," said Vinegar. "You expect it right back?"

"No. Please keep it a day or so. But do warn the boys who are . . . knotted up . . . that it is medicine, a potent and fast-working laxative." Mrs. Krickitt held up a pair of fingers. "Two tablespoons per dose, and only once a day. Pan Tin will measure it for you."

He left.

So did the three of us, by a roundabout route.

Micah and I, escorting Mrs. Krickitt between us, pretended to be airing an evening stroll; we did so in the general direction where our curiosity itched. Something was up. Because, in the vicinity of the bunkhouse, several assorted scenes of activity were unfolding. Mischief was there, invisible, like carbon monoxide.

Spout was loading two blood-red shells into a double-barrel shotgun. Spider, with a sly face, held a shovel. Domino was busy attaching a small bayonet to the lean end of a long bamboo fishing pole. Pointing to its sharp tip, he grinned.

"Needle," he whispered to Vinegar. "Go hide. But come running soon's you harken our signal."

Vinegar, still supervising his precious bottle of new acquired remedy, shuffled over to where Hoofrot was holding a mysterious shoe box.

Vin peeked inside and flinched.

Several men were whispering,

motioning, slinking here and yonder on
tiptoe. Some, having pulled off their boots,
were displaying stockings that had, a
decade ago, been white. I wondered what
prank they intended to play. Then I saw
where all of them seemed to concentrate.
Under a tree, a target by the name of
Jilly had removed only one boot and one
stocking that he held in his hand, and was
sleeping soundly. The sound was snoring.

"Ready?" Domino hissed.

"Now!" Hoofrot nodded, after emptying
a box of scorpions (which we later learned
were all dead) in a half circle around the
sleeping newcomer.

Just as Domino jabbed Jilly's naked foot
with the fishpole needle, Spout pulled on
both scattergun triggers.

WHAM . . .BANG.

The shotgun blasted up a storm of dust
around each of Jilly's hips. In ran Spider
to pound the ground with his shovel, as if
swatting the invaders.

CLANG . . .WOMP . . .CLANK.

"Scorpions!" several pokes hollered at
full voice.

Jumping up, Jilly grabbed his needle-
pricked foot and began to scream. "I got bit!
Oh, good merciful, I be bitten. One of them
deadly devils just bited me." He stomped a
dead scorpion with his boot.

"Can we save this poor sinner's life?"
Spout wailed.

Spider shook his head and made a
sorrowful face. "No use. Because once a
scorpy stings ya, you're nothing but a hard-
luck goner. Ain't it tragic?"

"Yup," agreed Hoofrot. "It's curtains."

"Wrong," cackled Vinegar, pretending to gallop from the bunkhouse. "There's hope. This'll save the misfortunate soul."

"Am I gonna die?" Jilly screeched.

"Nope," said Vinegar, "not if you drink this. It could spare your useless life. But you gotta swaller it down quick."

Jilly, not bothering to ask what medicinal miracle was in the bottle, lifted the Let Loose to his desperate lips and tipped up, gulping until the flask was empty.

"Run," Hoofrot told him. "It's your one chance to neutralizationize the poison. Run and jump. High as you can. And pray!"

It was a sight to behold.

Around and around the tree ran a petrified Jilly, jumping up and down, waving his arms, shouting what seemed closer to profanity than prayer. At least he mentioned God. In circles he ran and leaped, begging the Glory Forever to spare his life, until he could final run no more. Wet with sweat, he fell pathetic and panting to the ground.

As his face kissed the dust, we all crowded in for a more intimate squint.

Mr. Ornell Hopple, who usual kept himself aloof from pranksterism came too. Kneeling, our foreman rested a friendly hand on the patient.

"Whoa it easy, mister," Ornell said. He patted the fallen man's shoulder. "You're fixing to live," he said. "Jilly, maybe to your surprise, I'm keeping you on here. Dom reports that you're a able puncher. No need to doubt what my men tell me. Got it straight?"

Our newest hand nodded.

"You see," Mr. Hop continued, "we got us a zoo of folks on Spur Box, you included.

Try'n remember that it ain't a fault or a
weakness to git born a yeller Chinaman. Or
be black like Domino, whose face is sporting
a few white spots where the pigment quit
performing. Vinegar and me, we're olden,
and Hoofrot's gimpy lame."

"I understand, boss."

"If you gotta look down on somebody,
there's a ample supply of sorrowfuls in
The Bent Ace. Some are lazy. Others cheat
around a card table. Or pool table. They
got stinkers who abuse their horses, their
women, and even their kids. Now that's
low. Below what I scrape off my boot."

Jilly staggered to his feet. "Mr. Hop,
soon's I'm able I'll square myself with both
Tin Pan and Domino. That's a promise."

"Good man." Ornell winked at him. "If
you're fixing to call Spur Box a home, treat
her homely."

Be sure your prank gets people to laugh, not to cry.
Hurting someone isn't a valid prank. It's just cruelty. If
you derive pleasure from someone else's pain, you're a
rat, and you'll lead a lousy life. Rats live in sewers.

Pranks? Why is this chapter here? To illustrate to
you just *how* a clever caper can help to sharpen the
silhouette of a prankster.

A prank can charm an editor. And smile a reader.

Tickle me, Elmer.

S.F.C.

A typical movie.

In it, a cinematic cliché, a familiar scene you have seen scores of times.

The handsome hero Letch Libido and his sweetie Erotica are in a panic, fleeing from the bad people at full sprint. What happens? You can easily predict it because the Hollywood screenwriters include this cliché in every script. *Erotica trips and falls.*

Frowning, (her second of two facial expressions) she pretends pain while pretending a sprained ankle, then forgets which ankle she is supposed to touch.

Elmer Emerging, if you seriously plan to become an authentic author, please do this: In your cast, favor your readers with a genuine S.F.C.

Strong Female Character.

Here's one of the more enjoyable aspects of this profession—realizing you have conceived a S.F.C. to strengthen your story. Right now, do you wonder if I practice my preachery? Let's check a few of my novels.

Title	**S.F.C.**
Bro	Aunt Lulu
Cowboy Ghost	Mrs. Krickett
Extra Innings	Vidalia
Horse Thief	Doctor A.M. Platt
A Part of the Sky	Mama and Aunt Carrie

It will boost your writing ability if you give these leathery ladies a look. *Not* that I, the author, *describe* them as being steely and sturdy. No way! Because that would be *telling.*

Remember, good solid writing is *physics.* The uniting—and better yet, a head-to-head *clash* of elements. Without the marriage of sodium and chlorine, we won't beget *salt.* I repeat . . . physics. Tangibles are your target. It certain *ain't* "painting word pictures." So listen up to Doctor Peck.

A pro's prescription is seldom description.

Readers of my books will notice that the protagonists are usually male and my S.F.C.s play strong supporting roles. Why is that so? The answer is pig simple. I'm a man. It makes sense for me to write from the masculine perspective.

But, *Elvira* Emerging, the S.F.C. in your book may well be the protagonist with other characters, male and female, playing supporting roles. Whether as the main character or in a supporting role, the S.F.C. behaves with bowel. Guts. Physical acts are performed by them. Of equal importance, my S.F.C.

possesses *values* that help to build the backbone of a younger person.

In my own life there was an extremely Strong Female Character. My Aunt Ida in *Weeds In Bloom*. To wit:

>She lived uproad.
>Aunt Ida had resided in her tiny shack for near about all of her life. No amount of family persuasion could convince her to abandon the place. Or her independence.
>. . .near to everyone in the county talked about her, told stories about her adventures, and even whispered about some of her long-gone social activities. Rumor held that a century ago, in 1838, this particular Ida Peck had actual cocked back a musket hammer to full click, and, without aiming or sighting along the barrel, shot, wounded and killed a drunken half-crazed Saint Francis Indian by the name of Three Crows.
>At the time, she was only nine.
>Others said eight.
>All I knew was this: that even now, in spite of Aunt Ida's being well beyond a hundred, nobody ever considered molesting her with as much as a blink of bother. And that included the lowest types you could mention: tax assessors, revenue men, and judges. In her day, all of our Peck clan boasted, Aunt Ida knew how to still the very best whiskey out of sweet corn, water, and maple sugar. One swig would keep a lumberjack warm all winter, up until the middle of May.
>A few tongues wagged, remembering a time in her life she'd served in a county

jail. Not long, but long enough. A friendly
sheriff slid open the bars to her cell and
returned her to liberty. This was fair.
Because Ida had been imprisoned over a
very trivial matter. Nothing serious.

All she'd done was shoot a lawyer......

Aunt Ida could needlepoint an entire
Bible verse—"Jesus wept"—on a penny
button, butcher a hog (tame or wild), dig
up cure-all root (ginseng) and for people
fixing to sink a well she could locate an
underground vein of water by using a
divining rod of laurel wood.

Some said it was willow.

Ida Peck knew how to clog-dance, sing
over a hundred hymns from memory,
recite her own poetry, and quote from
almost every chapter in the Scriptures, Old
Testament or New.

She could neither read nor write.

One of the reasons that *Bro* was a successful novel is
the strong female character Aunt Lulu. In the following
scene, Aunt Lulu has arrived at the Yazoo police
station to take custody of her great-nephew, Tug,
whose parents have been killed in a violent accident.

Bro claimed everyone in Pecan County
was cautious of Aunt Lulu, including
gators, boar hogs, and sharks. Must be
the truth, because one glance made Chief
Percival Sweetbutter remove his cowboy
hat and give her a respectful bow.

"How do, Miss Dockery. I been in touch
with a Mr. Branch Dockery and—"

"Branch is my kid brother. He's only
seventy. We're two years apart, but not near

enough miles. That man is so cantankerous he'd piddle on a petunia."

She pointed at me. "Is this who I believe?"

The chief nodded. "Yes'm. Presume so. From all reports, this here youngster be Tugwell Dockery from up Georgia way. We've already identified their license plate. However, he is—"

"Save it." Aunt Lulu held up a halting hand, palm forward. "I've come to take full responsibility for him."

"Well now, according to law, Miss Dockery, and seeing that his parents are deceased and his brother is serving correctional time, the grandfather is legally next of kin, and thereby officially—"

"Ha! You can kiss my unofficial foot." She stomped her shoe. "Branch isn't fit to be put in charge of a dead rat. I trucked myself to the Pecan County prison, twice, to visit and console Broda Joe, this child's brother. He gave me a earful about Branch. That crusty old geezer hasn't been to see his grandson even a once." She raised a finger. "Not one time."

My advice to all writers—never ignore the granite gal in your stories. Strong Female Characters add fiber to your fiction.

Paddle Upstream

Work.

It's hard work.

So much easier, isn't it, merely to float downstream without any effort? But that's not *how* your story progresses. Mine never does.

Picture a map of the forty-eight states. Where are you? New Orleans, Louisiana, and you're fixing to paddle a canoe upstream. Due north. However, this is not a trip through a canal that has walls on both banks and no decisions to make. Your canoe is your story. But as you paddle up the Mississippi, there are many alternatives. Several routes to follow. A wealth of waterways. Rivers galore, and lucky you!

On your right, there's the Homochitto, Big Black, Ohio, Allegheny, Monogahela. To your left, you'll find the Arkansas, Missouri, Des Moines, Kansas, Platt, Powder, and Big Muddy.

What's my point?

When you start your northbound journey at New Orleans, or when you begin your books, *you never know* in advance where you'll end up. The mountains in western New York State or Montana.

We authors are not supposed to know prematurely. Because if *we* know, then the plot is too obvious and our readers will know too. Besides, when I'm writing a book, I can seldom foresee where it's going. Honest. A *character*, not an author, will eventually determine the book's destination.

This particular character may be acting out of strength, or weakness. But he *must want.* Then *do* something to direct the plot's upstream course.

As you write your own adventure, this reasoning shall fall neatly into place and make sense. And please don't fret over a few wrong turns. You can always *erase* . . . by that, I mean you'll turn your canoe around, return to the Mississippi, again go north to explore another tributary. And another. Until you get somewhere exciting. I hope you run into troublesome danger.

The secret is hard work.

So keep paddling.

Fan Mail

First off, thanks!

Every published author ought to feel grateful for
friendly letters and all those gray USPS bags in which
they arrive. Many bring mirth. To wit . . .

> *Mr. Peck,*
> *I read your book. My teacher made me*
> *do it.*

> *Dear Mr. Peck,*
> *At school, we read authors that are both*
> *alive and dead. If you're no longer alive,*
> *don't bother to answer.*

A critic wrote to me.

> *Mr. Peck:*
> *I reviewed your last novel. Let's all hope*
> *it is your last.*

Most of the letters I receive are mercifully brief,
thank goodness, as the older I grow, the more
valuable time becomes.
Helpful hints:

1. Please send all group letters flat (unfolded) in
   one package with a short covering letter from
   a teacher or prof.

2. Include a SASE.

3. Group letters from a *school* get immediate attention.

In conclusion, please allow a repeating of my gratefulness to every reader who takes the time and effort to contact me. *How* flattering that a number have suggested that I run for president of the United States. But after cautious consideration, I do not choose to run, and here's why.

All those letters were written in Crayola.

There's only one way to close this chapter. It is sharing with you a most sincere yet amusing tribute that any author would forever cherish. It began with "Hi Rob" and ended with "Your pal, Charley." In between, only seven sterling words.

"I like your books better than literature."

Last Gasp

In closing, a few figs from a thistle.

Why is this chapter added? For good reason. Because
your author is not an omniscient deity but rather
a human being. Like yours, my gums bleed when I
floss. Sometimes I net an easy tennis overhead. And
often drive a golf ball into woods, water, or sand.

A writer's duty is to be up-front *honest*. To inform
y'all, as the saying goes, as to where I'm coming
from. And what makes me tick.

I am seventy-eight years old, living proof that the
good die young.

Here are some parting shots about what little
I've learned in life. Perhaps more wisecrack than
wisdom. Shells one stoops to collect during
a barefoot walk on the sharp-stoned beach of
experience. So please allow me to open up and
welcome you inside my mind and heart.

I respect a man who's been a soldier or a sailor.

Dealing with people, beware the quiet dog. Within
him lurks a fangy and ferocious cat.

Never equate education and virtue. Education earns you a living. Virtue shines your soul. And warms those around you.

If a whale had a thumb, he'd rule the world? No, he'd hitchhike.

When a child is rude, spank its parents.

Ignore criticism. If a stable boy hurls a horse turd at a king's carriage, the king is unaware. The hurler has nothing but a brown hand.

The best prayers are wordlessly watching a dawn or a sunset.

Dull minds complicate an issue. Sharp minds simplify.

It's never too late for senility. Someday soon, age will bestow a final benevolence and allow me once again to be a child.